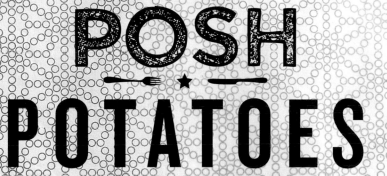

POSH POTATOES

Over 70 recipes,
from wondrous waffles to fabulous fries

Rebecca Woods

Photography by Faith Mason

Hardie Grant

QUADRILLE

Publishing Director: Sarah Lavelle
Series Designer: Gemma Hayden
Designer: Katherine Keeble
Food Stylist and Recipe Writer: Rebecca Woods
Photographer: Faith Mason
Props Stylist: Alexander Breeze
Production Controller: Katie Jarvis
Production Director: Vincent Smith

Published in 2019 by Quadrille,
an imprint of Hardie Grant Publishing

Quadrille
52–54 Southwark Street
London SE1 1UN
quadrille.com

Cataloguing in Publication Data: a catalogue
record for this book is available from the
British Library.

ISBN: 978 1 78713 357 0

Printed in China

CONTENTS

—☆—

★

INTRODUCTION

Ah, potatoes, the true gold of the new world. Their inherent brilliantness makes you wonder why the conquistadors bothered about the other, shinier stuff. So wonderful are they, that you can find potato in food cultures the world over, and given these international makeovers, the humble spud can be a lot fancier than you might think. Sure, there's a time and a place when a simple baked potato topped with a lump of melting butter is all you could ever wish for, but it's time to embrace their somewhat posher incarnations, too.

But one potato is certainly not the same as the next; they all have their own different characters – pick the right one for the job and you can't go too far wrong. A couple of simple things to remember: look for floury ones for mashing and roasting, when light and fluffy is the aim; for salads, boiled or steamed potatoes, or when you need them to hold their own a bit more (say, in a stew), go for a waxy variety. And never overlook the wonderful sweet potato as yet another option.

And a final word of endorsement – while they get a pretty bad rap healthwise, they are actually a decent source of vitamins and minerals, as well as being rich in fibre, if you eat the skins. Okay, perhaps dauphinoise isn't an everyday dinner… but they have more going for them than just their flavour, their versatility, their economy, their availability, their ease of cooking and their status as a Class A comfort food. Super spuds don't always have to be the supporting artist – they can be the star too.

BASIC

★

MASHED POTATO

Lovely as they are, or use them as a base for many
of the other recipes in this book, such as for breakfast
in bread (see page 36), or wrapped around delicious
fillings and fried (see page 48).

SERVES 4

TAKES 25 minutes

1kg (2lb 4oz) floury potatoes,
   peeled and quartered (cut any
   really large ones down a bit
   more so they are all about the
   same size)
50g (1¾oz/3½ tbsp) butter,
   softened and diced
3 tbsp whole milk
sea salt and freshly ground
   black pepper

Put the potatoes in a pan and cover generously
with cold water. Add a good few pinches of salt
to the water. Set the pan over a high heat and bring
the water to the boil. Once boiling, turn the heat
down to medium, pop a lid on the pan and leave
the potatoes to simmer for 15 minutes or so, until
they are tender and the point of a sharp knife can
be easily inserted.

Drain the potatoes and return them to the hot pan.
Add the butter and milk and mash until smooth
with a potato masher. (Never attempt to do this in
a food processor – you will end up with something
akin to wallpaper paste.) Season well with salt and
pepper and serve hot.

BAKED

★

POTATOES

The simplest, but possibly most satisfying, way to enjoy
potatoes – perhaps because of the lack of effort required.
See the filling suggestions below, or use your imagination to
personalize your pots.

SERVES as many as you like

TAKES 1½ hours

as many baking potatoes as
   you need – 1 per person
sea salt and freshly ground
   black pepper
butter, to serve

Preheat the oven to 180ºC/350ºF/gas 4.

Put the potatoes in the oven and bake for about
1–1½ hours, depending on their size, or until tender
throughout when pierced with a knife.

And that's it.

Well, you could speed things up by starting them
off in a microwave, and then crisping up the skin in
the oven, if you're in a hurry. But the skins are nicer
when cooked in the oven from the get-go.

Simply slice the potatoes into quarters, not cutting
all the way through, let a good dollop of butter
melt into the middle of each, and serve.

Or try one of the filling suggestions below...
• Classic baked beans, with cheese melted on top
• Leeks in cheese sauce (with or without bacon)
• Tuna mayonnaise – add spring onions (scallions),
peppers, corn, or whatever veggies you fancy to up
the healthy stakes
• Garlic mushrooms and blue cheese
• Go retro with prawns and Marie Rose sauce
• Chilli con carne (or sweet potato and bean chilli –
see page 162) and sour cream

11

CLASSIC
★
ROAST POTATOES

Sunday lunch wouldn't be complete without these.
But you can dispense with all those fancy duck or goose fat
versions – for the crispiest roasties, you can't beat plain old
sunflower oil.

🍴 SERVES 4

⏰ TAKES 50 minutes

1kg (2lb 4oz) floury potatoes (such
as Maris Piper, King Edward, or
even baking potatoes)
sunflower oil, for roasting

Peel the potatoes and chop them into large chunks.
Put them in a pan of cold, salted water and bring
to the boil. Once boiling, parboil the potatoes for
8 minutes or so, until softening around the edges
but still a little firm in the middle.

Meanwhile preheat the oven to 200ºC/400ºF/
gas 6. Pour enough oil into a large baking tray to
thinly cover the bottom. Put the tray in the oven
to heat up for a few minutes. The trick to crispy
roasties is getting the tray and the oil really hot
so they don't have a chance to go soggy.

Once cooked, drain the potatoes in a colander and
leave them to steam dry for a minute or so. Tip the
potatoes back into the saucepan and pop the lid
on. Using oven gloves as the pan will still be quite
hot, hold the lid on the pan and shake it up and
down firmly a few times to rough up the potatoes a
little. Don't go too mad or they'll begin to break up.

Take the tray of hot oil out of the oven and arrange
the potatoes in the tray, turning them over in the
oil as you go so they are well coated. Return the
tray to the oven and roast for about 40 minutes,
turning halfway through cooking, until they are
golden brown and crispy all over.

ROASTED NEW POTATOES ★
WITH GARLIC & ROSEMARY

You can just leave these plain, and they can be served with pretty much anything, but this flavour combo is delicious. The garlic goes lovely and toasty, but make sure it's added towards the end as it can turn bitter if it burns.

SERVES 4

TAKES 40 minutes

1kg (2lb 4oz) new potatoes, diced
    into 1.5cm (⅔in) chunks
3 tbsp olive oil
3 large garlic cloves, finely
    chopped
1 heaped tbsp finely chopped
    rosemary needles
sea salt flakes

Preheat the oven to 180ºC/350ºF/gas 4.

Tip the diced potatoes into a baking tray and drizzle with the olive oil. Sprinkle with sea salt flakes, then stir everything together well. Put the tray in the oven and roast for 25 minutes, until the potatoes are almost tender and beginning to take on some colour.

Sprinkle the chopped garlic and the rosemary evenly over the potatoes and stir in. Return the pan to the oven for 10 minutes more until everything is golden. Serve hot.

CHIPS OR

★

FRIES

Not only a classic side for fish, these can be made into unexpected and rather different feasts – see Lomo Saltado (page 170). The two (or even three, if you're Belgian) stage cooking process is a must for the crispiest chips.

SERVES 4

TAKES 20 minutes, plus soaking

1kg (2lb 4oz) floury potatoes
vegetable oil, for frying
sea salt

Peel the potatoes and cut them into 1cm (½in) thick batons. Put them in a colander and rinse them really well under running water. If you have time, leave them to soak in water for a couple of hours to remove as much starch as possible – this will make them crispier. Once soaked and rinsed, dry them as well as you can with kitchen paper or a clean tea towel.

Meanwhile, heat the oil in a frying pan with a thermometer or in a deep fat fryer to 130ºC/250ºF. Pop the chips in and cook for about 7 minutes, until almost completely tender, but not coloured at all. Drain them on kitchen paper and leave to cool. You can do this stage a good few hours in advance, or even the night before if you like.

When you are almost ready to serve, turn the heat up and get the oil to 190ºC/375ºF. This time you'll need to cook in two or three batches as the crisps won't get crispy if you overcrowd the pan. Cook the chips for 3–4 minutes, or until golden and crisp. Drain on kitchen paper and season with salt before serving.

★

GNOCCHI

The key to this is not adding too much flour, and not working the mixture once it's combined so that the gluten in the flour isn't developed too much. This will give you the lightest, fluffiest gnocchi.

SERVES 4

TAKES 2 hours

3 large baking potatoes (1kg/2lb 4oz total weight)
150g (5½oz/1 heaped cup) plain (all-purpose) flour, plus extra for dusting
sea salt

Preheat the oven to 180ºC/350ºF/gas 4.

Prick the potatoes with a fork a few times and bake for 1–1½ hours, until tender throughout. Remove from the oven and slice them in half. Being careful not to burn yourself, although this should be done when the potatoes are reasonably hot, scoop the cooked potato flesh from the skins and put it in a mixing bowl. Mash until really smooth, then sift in the flour and season with salt. Fold together gently until just combined; if you work the mixture too much the gnocchi will end up being chewy.

On a floured surface, roll about one-quarter of the mixture into a long sausage about 1.5cm (⅔in) thick. Slice the sausage into 2cm (¾in) lengths, then roll them across the back of a fork to make grooves in the dough. Place the gnocchi on a flour-dusted tray, and repeat with the remaining potato mixture.

To cook the gnocchi, get a large pan of salted water boiling. Working in batches so you don't overcrowd the pan, throw in a couple of handfuls of gnocchi. Wait for it to rise to the surface, then count to 15 before fishing it out with a slotted spoon. Allow the water to return to the boil before adding the next batch. Continue until all the gnocchi is cooked.

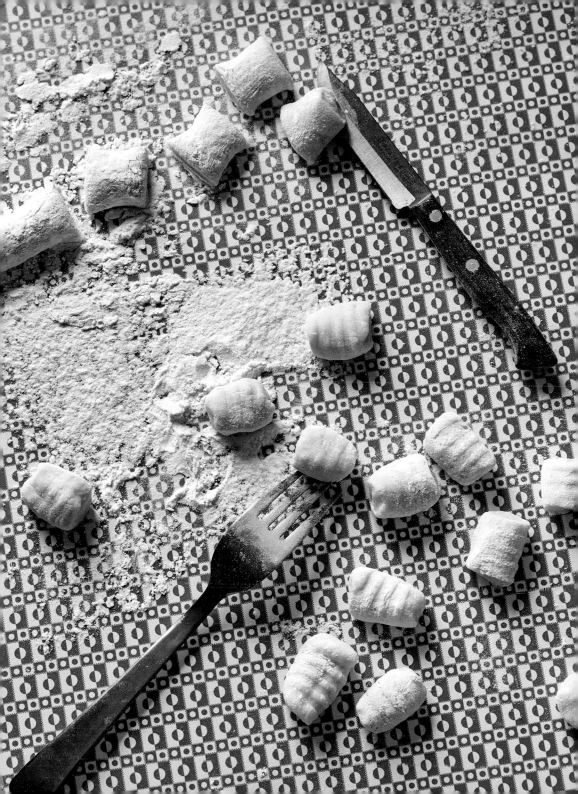

BREAKFAST & BRUNCH

★

POTATOES

POTATO, KALE &

★

CORNED BEEF HASH

A brilliant, economical, satisfying dish that's well overdue
to come back into fashion.

SERVES 2

TAKES 25 minutes

500g (1lb 2oz) floury potatoes,
   peeled and diced into 1.5cm
   (⅔in) cubes
2 tbsp olive oil, plus a little extra
   to fry the eggs
½ onion, sliced
150g (5½oz) kale, thick stalks
   discarded and roughly chopped
1 tbsp Worcestershire sauce
1 small can (130g/4½oz) corned
   beef
2 eggs
sea salt and freshly ground black
   pepper

Put the potatoes in a pan of boiling, salted water
and bring the water back up to the boil. Cook for
about 5 minutes, until beginning to soften but still
holding together. Drain and leave them to steam
dry in the colander.

Meanwhile, heat the oil in a frying pan over
low–medium heat and add the onion. Cook
for 5 minutes until softened. Add the kale and
Worcestershire sauce, pop a lid on the pan and
continue to cook for about 5 minutes, until the
kale has wilted. Add the cubed potato and cook for
about 8 minutes more, uncovered, until the potato
has browned. Keep watch and move the potato
around so it cooks evenly.

Add the corned beef to the pan and stir in. Season
with salt and pepper and leave over a low heat to
warm the beef through while you sort out the eggs.

Drizzle a bit of oil into a non-stick frying pan
and heat over a medium heat. Crack the eggs into
the pan and cook over a medium heat for about
3 minutes, until the whites are set but the yolks
are still runny. Divide the hash between two plates,
pop an egg on top of each, season and serve hot.

HERBY HASH BROWNS ★
WITH EGGS & MACKEREL

Fresh herbs add a lovely twist to this classic breakfast dish, and make them a great base for fish, as here, served topped with scrambled eggs and smoked mackerel.

SERVES 4

TAKES 25 minutes

450g (1lb) potatoes (such as small–
   medium sized Maris Piper or
   Désirée), whole and unpeeled
1 egg, beaten
1 tbsp plain (all-purpose) flour
2 large handfuls of fresh herbs
   (tarragon, dill, chives, parsley,
   soft thyme, whatever you have
   to hand), stripped from their
   stalks and roughly chopped
½ tsp sea salt, or to taste
1 tbsp butter
1 tbsp vegetable oil
scrambled eggs, to serve (optional)
250g (9oz) smoked mackerel,
   flaked into large chunks
freshly ground black pepper

Put the potatoes in a pan of cold, salted water and bring to the boil. Turn the heat down to a simmer and cook for about 8 minutes, until starting to soften but still quite firm. Drain and leave to cool a little in the colander.

Once the potatoes are cool enough to handle, grate them into a large bowl (leave the skin on, it adds flavour). Pour in the beaten egg and add the flour, herbs and salt. Stir until everything is well combined. Shape the mixture into 4 patties.

Melt the butter in a large non-stick frying pan with the vegetable oil and set over a medium heat. Once hot, add the patties (you may need to cook them in batches) and cook for 3–4 minutes on each side, until golden. Remove from the pan with a slotted spoon and transfer to plates.

Serve the hash browns topped with scrambled eggs flaked mackerel, and plenty of black pepper.

BOXING DAY
★
BUBBLE & SQUEAK

Try to rein in the gluttony on Christmas day and you won't
just avoid indigestion but also have leftovers to make this.
All quantities are approximate – you just need to make sure
you've got enough starchy fare to bind it all together.

🍴 SERVES 2–4

⏰ TAKES 25 minutes

1 tbsp olive oil
20g (⅔oz/1½ tbsp) butter
1 small onion, finely sliced
8–10 leftover roast potato chunks
5–6 leftover roast parsnip chunks
a couple of slices of leftover
    turkey, shredded
a few crispy smoked bacon slices
    or a thick slice of gammon (or
    ham), shredded
a large handful of leftover cooked
    carrot slices
8 leftover cooked Brussels sprouts,
    quartered
sea salt and freshly ground black
    pepper
cranberry sauce, to serve

Heat the oil and butter in a largeish non-stick frying
pan over low–medium heat until the butter has
melted. Add the onion and cook for a good 5–10
minutes until is really softened. Add the potatoes
and parsnips and use a potato masher to mash
them in the pan to a rough, chunky mash (turn the
heat off while you do the mashing).

Add the turkey, bacon, carrots and Brussels sprouts
to the pan, along with some salt and pepper (how
much will depend on how much you seasoned
everything the day before), and mix everything
together, then press the mixture down gently until
it's compacted into one large patty. Cook for about
6 minutes, until the bottom of the patty has turned
a golden brown.

Carefully, and using oven gloves, place a plate on
top of the pan and invert the patty onto the plate.
Slide it back into the pan and cook for a further 6
minutes or so, until the other side is golden brown
and it's piping hot throughout.

Serve hot with a dollop of cranberry sauce.

GRIDDLED POTATO FARLS
★
WITH SLOW-ROAST TOMATOES

The less flour you put in, the fluffier these farls are, so light
and gentle (on a well-floured surface) is the key to rolling
them out so the soft dough isn't glued to the worktop.

SERVES 4–6

TAKES 1 hour

For the farls:
1kg (2lb 4oz) floury potatoes
40g (1½oz/2½ tbsp) butter, melted
120g (4oz/scant 1 cup) plain
    (all-purpose) flour, plus plenty
    more for dusting
1 tsp flaky sea salt

For the tomatoes:
6 large tomatoes
2 tbsp olive oil
a drizzle of balsamic vinegar
leaves stripped from a few sprigs
    of thyme
1 tsp soft brown sugar
sea salt and freshly ground black
    pepper

Preheat the oven to 170°C/325°F/gas 3. Slice the
tomatoes in half and place them, cut side up, in a
baking tray. Drizzle with the oil and a little balsamic,
then sprinkle with the thyme and sugar. Season
well, then roast for 1 hour, until well softened.

Meanwhile, put the potatoes in a pan of salted
water and bring to the boil. Once boiling, cook
for about 15 minutes, or until tender. Drain and let
them steam dry in the colander for a couple of
minutes, before tipping back into the hot pan and
mashing, with the butter, until smooth. Carefully
fold in the flour and salt until just combined.

Heavily dust a work surface. Divide the dough into
four equal portions and shape the first one into a
ball. Roll it out gently to a circle about 5mm (¼in)
thick. Repeat to make four circles. Cut each circle
into quarters, so you have 16 wedges.

Preheat a griddle pan to very hot over a high heat
(no need to grease it). Place as many wedges on the
pan as you can and cook for about 3 minutes, until
dark griddle lines are beginning to appear. Flip them
over and cook for another 3 minutes on the other
side. Repeat in as many batches as you need to
cook the remaining dough.

Serve the farls hot, topped with roasted tomatoes.

SHAKSHUKA WITH
★
POTATOES & CHORIZO

Adding potatoes makes this classic Middle Eastern-style brunch a little more satisfying, and removes the need to it serve with bread. Leave out the chorizo to make it vegetarian – it will still be delicious.

SERVES 4

TAKES 50 minutes

400g (14oz) baby new potatoes, halved, or quertered if large
2 tbsp olive oil, plus extra if needed
1 onion, finely sliced
2 garlic cloves, finely chopped
1 red (bell) pepper, deseeded and sliced
1 yellow or orange (bell) pepper, deseeded and sliced
100g (3½oz) chorizo, diced (optional)
¼–½ tsp dried chilli (hot pepper) flakes
1 tsp ground cumin
1 tsp ground coriander
2 tsp sweet smoked paprika
1 x 400g (14oz) can chopped tomatoes
4 eggs
sea salt and ground black pepper
thick yogurt, to serve
small handful of flat-leaf parsley leaves, to serve

Cook the potatoes in a pan of salted water until tender but still quite firm – about a minute or so off being perfectly done. Drain them and let them steam dry in the colander for a few minutes.

Heat the olive oil in a large non-stick sauté pan with a lid over high heat and add the potatoes. Cook for about 5 minutes until turning golden, then remove them from the pan with a slotted spoon.

Add a little more oil to the pan if needs be. Turn the heat down to medium–low, add the onion to the pan and cook for 5 minutes until softening. Add the garlic, peppers, chorizo, if using, and spices and cook for 5 minutes more until the peppers are softening. Add the chopped tomatoes and swill out the can with about 80ml (2½fl oz/⅓ cup) water, and tip that in too. Simmer for 15 minutes until everything is cooked and tender. Taste and season.

Stir the potatoes into the sauce, then make 4 wells in the mixture. Crack an egg into each one and pop the lid on the pan. Cook for 6–7 minutes, or until the egg whites are set but the yolks are still runny.

Drizzle a little yogurt over the shakshuka, then sprinkle with parsley and serve in the pan.

POTATOES

★

O'BRIEN

This is an American classic (with a little liberty taken with the Worcestershire sauce to add a bit more flavour) that's great alongside eggs, bacon, mushrooms, baked beans, or any other breakfast favourites.

SERVES 4

TAKES 30 minutes

30g (1oz/2 tbsp) butter
2 tbsp olive oil
800g (1lb 12oz) new potatoes, cut
    into 1.5cm (⅔in) cubes
2 small (or 1 very large) red onion,
    finely sliced
1 large garlic clove, finely chopped
1 red (bell) pepper, deseeded and
    cut into stamp-sized dice
1 green (bell) pepper, deseeded
    and cut into stamp-sized dice
1 tbsp Worcestershire sauce
sea salt and freshly ground
    black pepper

Melt the butter with the oil in a large sauté pan over medium–low heat and add the potatoes. Put the lid on and cook for about 15 minutes, stirring occasionally, until beginning to soften and pick up colour. Add the onions, garlic and peppers and cook for another 10 minutes, leaving the lid off this time, until the potatoes and peppers are soft and the onions are wilted and translucent.

Add the Worcestershire sauce to the pan, turn up the heat to medium–high and cook for 5 minutes more until most of the moisture from the sauce has cooked off and the flavours are all mingling together. Taste and season generously with salt and pepper, then serve with whichever breakfast accompaniments you wish.

POTATO PANCAKE STACK
★
WITH BACON & MAPLE

A crowd-pleaser if ever there was one, adding potato to these helps them feel a little more substantial – but don't worry, they're still light and fluffy.

🍴 SERVES 4

⏱ TAKES 30 minutes

350g (12oz) floury potatoes, cut into large chunks
175ml (5½fl oz/¾ cup) whole milk
2 eggs, beaten
100g (3½oz/¾ cup) plain (all-purpose) flour
1 tsp baking powder
sea salt
butter, for frying
12 slices smoked streaky bacon
maple syrup, to serve

Put the potatoes in a pan of water and bring to the boil. Cook for about 15 minutes, until tender when pierced with a knife, then drain and return them to the hot pan. Add a good splash of the milk and mash to a smooth purée, as lump-free as possible. Add the remaining milk and the eggs and beat until well combined.

Fold the flour, baking powder and a pinch of salt into the mixture until all the flour has been evenly incorporated, but try not to overmix.

Melt a little butter in a large non-stick frying pan over a low–medium heat and add a ladleful of batter to the pan per pancake. (You'll need to cook them in batches.) Cook for 2 minutes, until the top looks firm enough to turn over, and the bottom is golden brown. Flip them over and cook for another 2 minutes on the other side, then remove from the pan and keep warm while you cook the rest.

While the pancakes are cooking, grab another large frying pan. Add the bacon and fry over a high heat until brown and crisp.

Serve the stacks of pancakes topped with bacon and finished with a good drizzle of maple syrup.

LEFTOVER MASH &

★

ROSEMARY BREAD

This makes a brilliant brekkie toasted, buttered and drizzled with honey. Potato gives it a lovely texture and flavour, almost sourdough-like.

MAKES 1 loaf

TAKES 1¾ hours

350g (12oz/3¼ cups) strong white bread flour
1 x 7g (¼oz) sachet instant yeast
1 tsp fine sea salt
2 tsp caster (superfine) sugar
1 tbsp finely chopped rosemary leaves
100ml (3½fl oz/scant ½ cup) warm water
125ml (4fl oz/½ cup) warm whole milk
200g (7oz) Mashed Potato (see page 8)
oil, for greasing
butter and honey, to serve

Put the flour in the bowl of a stand mixer and make a well in the middle. Sprinkle in the yeast, salt, sugar and rosemary. Add the water, milk and mashed potato and knead with a dough hook for 10 minutes, or until the dough is smooth and elastic. Grease a large bowl with a little oil and transfer the dough to the bowl, turning it over so it's coated on all sides with the oil. Cover with cling film (plastic wrap) and leave to prove in a warm place for 30 minutes, or until doubled in size. Meanwhile, grease a long 900g (2lb) bread tin (pan).

Once the dough has risen, turn it out of the bowl and knead briefly to knock out the air. Shape it into a loaf roughly the same shape as the tin and drop it in. Cover with a piece of greased cling film and leave to rise again until doubled in size.

While the bread is on its second prove, preheat the oven to 200°C/400°F/gas 6 and put a large roasting pan in the bottom of the oven to heat up.

Once proved, put the bread in the oven, adding a cup of water to the hot roasting pan at the same time. Bake for 30–35 minutes, until golden, risen and sounding hollow when tapped on the base.

Leave the bread to cool before slicing. Serve toasted, buttered and drizzled with honey.

POTATO WAFFLES WITH
★
ELDERFLOWER PEACHES

Bird's Eye has got nothing on these, fresh from the waffle iron. Serve with charred, elderflower-infused peaches for a super-sweet summer brekkie.

SERVES 4

TAKES 30 minutes,
plus marinating time

For the waffles:
750g (1lb 10oz) floury potatoes,
   peeled and halved
45g (1½oz/3 tbsp) butter, softened
2 eggs
3 tbsp plain (all-purpose) flour

For the peaches:
6 ripe peaches, stoned and each
   cut into 6 wedges
80ml (2½fl oz/⅓ cup) good-quality
   elderflower cordial

To serve:
raspberries
Greek yogurt
honey

Put the peaches in a shallow bowl and pour over the elderflower cordial. Leave them to marinate for an hour or two (the longer the better), stirring occasionally.

Meanwhile, put the potatoes in a pan of cold water and bring to the boil. Boil for 15 minutes, or until tender. Drain well, then tip them back into the hot pan. Add the butter and mash them really well until smooth. Beat in the egg thoroughly, then gently fold in the flour until just combined.

Preheat a waffle iron with non-stick plates to medium–high. Preheat a griddle pan until very hot.

Spoon half of the mixture into the hot waffle iron, piling it more in the middle as it will be pushed out to the sides once the lid is shut. Cook for 5 minutes until golden brown and holding together. Carefully remove the waffle and keep it warm while you cook the second half of the mixture.

While you cook the waffles, griddle the peaches for about 4 minutes, turning halfway through, until charred on both sides.

Arrange the waffles on plates and top with the peaches, a few raspberries, blobs of yogurt and a drizzle of honey.

SPICED & SEEDED
★
SWEET POTATO MUFFINS

These have so many lovely breakfast ingredients in them – oats, fruit, yogurt, seeds, eggs – with the bonus of sweet potato, adding sweetness and making them lovely and moist. Best served warm, fresh from the oven.

 MAKES 12

TAKES 45 minutes

1 very large sweet potato
  (about 450g/1lb)
150g (5½oz/⅔ cup) butter,
  melted and cooled
150g (5½oz/scant ⅔ cup)
  natural yogurt
4 tbsp whole milk
2 large eggs, lightly beaten
2 tsp vanilla extract
250g (9oz/1¾ cups) plain
  (all-purpose) flour
120g (4oz/1 heaped cup)
  porridge oats
150g (5½oz/¾ cup) soft
  brown sugar
2 tsp baking powder
1 tsp bicarbonate of soda
  (baking soda)
3 tsp ground cinnamon
2 tsp ground ginger
140g (5oz/1 cup) raisins
130g (4½oz/1 cup) mixed seeds

Preheat oven to 170°C/325°F/gas 3 and line a muffin tray with 12 muffin cases.

Cook the potato in the microwave for 10–12 minutes, or until tender throughout. Scoop out the cooked flesh into a bowl and mash well – you need about 300g (10oz) cooked flesh. Add the butter, yogurt, milk, eggs and vanilla, and beat until you have a smooth, lump-free mixture.

In another large bowl, combine the flour, oats, sugar, baking powder, bicarbonate of soda (baking soda), cinnamon, ginger, raisins and three-quarters of the mixed seeds.

Pour the liquid ingredients into the dry ones and fold together to combine well, but don't overwork the mixture. Divide the batter between the 12 muffin cases, and sprinkle the top of each with a few of the remaining mixed seeds.

Pop the tray in the oven and bake for about 25 minutes, until well risen, golden and a knife inserted into the middle of one of the muffins comes out clean. Leave to cool for 5 minutes in the tray, then serve warm, or transfer to a wire rack and leave to cool completely.

LUNCH

★

POTATOES

SOUR CREAM & CHIVE

★

BAKED POTATO SOUP

You might ask, why bother spending the time baking the potatoes? Well, the golden crispy skin is what gives this soup it's lovely toasty flavour. Although, as ever, the cheese doesn't hurt, either.

 SERVES 4–6

TAKES 1½ hours

750g (1lb 10oz) baking potatoes
15g (1 tbsp) butter
1 tbsp olive oil
1 onion, finely sliced
1 garlic clove, finely diced
800ml (28fl oz/3½ cups)
   vegetable stock
150ml (5fl oz/scant ⅔ cup)
   sour cream
bunch of fresh chives, snipped
sea salt and freshly ground
   black pepper
grated or diced cheese (cubes of
   Taleggio are great with this),
   to serve (optional)

Preheat the oven to 180ºC/350ºF/gas 4. Bake the potatoes for 1–1½ hours, or until tender.

Meanwhile, melt the butter with the oil in a large saucepan and add the onion. Fry for 5 minutes or until softened and translucent, then add the garlic and fry for a couple of minutes more. Pour in the stock and heat until simmering.

Once the potatoes are cooked, roughly chop them and add to the saucepan, skins and all. Transfer the mixture to a blender and blitz until almost smooth. It doesn't matter if there are flecks of the skin showing in the mixture – they add character.

Add the sour cream and blitz briefly to combine, then tip the soup back into the pan. Season to taste and reheat the soup until hot. Stir in most of the snipped chives just before serving.

Ladle the soup into bowls and top with grated or diced cheese (if liked) and a sprinkle of the reserved chives.

HOT POTATO, CHORIZO &
★
PEPPER SALAD

This is a salad born out of idleness; one roasting tray, a few bits and bobs from the fridge and enough glugs of olive oil that the whole thing becomes self-saucing (well, self-dressing).

SERVES 4

TAKES 45 minutes

500g (1lb 2oz) small new potatoes (skin on), halved or quartered if much bigger than a walnut

3 tbsp olive oil, plus more if needed

1 tsp sweet smoked paprika

1 red (bell) pepper, halved and deseeded

140g (5oz) chorizo, sliced into half moons

1 tbsp good-quality sherry vinegar

80g (2¾oz/¾ cup) pitted black or Kalamata olives

80g (2¾oz/1 cup) sun-blushed tomatoes, roughly chopped

120g (4oz) wild rocket (arugula) leaves

sea salt flakes and freshly ground black pepper

Preheat the oven to 180°C/350°F/gas 4.

Put potatoes in a roasting tray and drizzle with the olive oil. Sprinkle with the paprika and a good pinch of salt and stir together so everything is well coated. Roast for 20 minutes.

Add the pepper to the roasting tray, stir to coat in the oil and return to the oven for a further 10 minutes. Add the chorizo and cook for a final 10 minutes.

Transfer the potatoes, chorizo and pepper to a salad bowl with a slotted spoon, leaving the oil. Add the sherry vinegar to the oil in the tray and taste. If it's too vinegary for your taste, add another 1 tbsp olive oil. Season with more salt, if needed, and a little black pepper.

Add the olives, tomatoes and rocket (arugula) to the salad bowl with the cooked ingredients. Drizzle with the dressing in the tray, toss everything together and serve immediately.

PAPA

★

RELLENA

The Peruvians know how to celebrate the humble spud, and so these delicious stuffed potato croquettes are shaped to look like potatoes. The filling is best made the day before, so it is completely cool and more flavourful.

🍴 MAKES 12

⏰ TAKES 1¼ hours, plus cooling time

1.4kg (3lb 2oz) floury potatoes, peeled and cut into chunks
2 egg yolks, plus 2 beaten eggs for coating
plain (all-purpose) flour, for dusting
120g (4oz/heaped 1 cup) dried breadcrumbs
sunflower or vegetable oil, for frying

For the filling:
2 tbsp olive oil
1 small onion, finely diced
1 garlic clove, finely chopped
200g (7oz) minced (ground) beef
1 tsp ground cumin
2 tsp fresh chilli paste
200g (7oz) chopped canned tomatoes (½ x 400g/14oz can)
1 heaped tsp tomato purée (paste)

First make the filling. Heat the oil in a saucepan over a low–medium heat and add the onion and garlic. Cook for 6 minutes or so, until the onion is softened and translucent. Add the mince and cook for a few minutes more until browned.

Add the cumin, chilli paste, chopped tomatoes and tomato purée (paste) and stir in. Put a lid on the pan and let it cook away for about 10 minutes, stirring occasionally in case it starts to stick. Remove the lid and add the olives and raisins and let it cook for 5–10 minutes more, until all the liquid has gone and the mixture is thick. Taste and season with salt and pepper, then leave to cool.

Meanwhile, boil the egg for 9½ minutes, until hard-boiled. Run under cold running water to cool quickly, then peel and chop. Once the meat mixture has cooled, stir in the chopped boiled egg.

Put the potatoes in a pan of cold, salted water and bring to the boil. Boil for 15–18 minutes, or until tender and a knife can be inserted easily. Drain well, then tip them back into the hot pan and mash them thoroughly. Once smooth and cooled down a little stir in the egg yolks until well incorporated and season with salt and pepper.

★ ★

PAPA RELLENA
continued...

35g (1¼oz/⅓ cup) green olives,
   roughly chopped
35g (1¼oz/¼ cup) raisins
1 large egg
sea salt and freshly ground
   black pepper

Put the oil in a saucepan and heat it to 180°C/
350°F. Put the flour on a plate, the eggs in a shallow
bowl and the breadcrumbs on another plate.

Divide the potato and meat filling each into roughly
12 portions. Take a portion of the potato and press
it out on your hand (you may want to dust your
hand with flour first), then put a portion of filling
in the middle. Fold the potato up around the filling
and smooth over to cover the filling completely,
shaping it into an oval-ish potato shape as you go.
Repeat until you have 12 balls.

One at a time, dip the balls into the flour,
then cover in the egg, then coat completely in
breadcrumbs. Repeat, dipping just in the egg again
and then the crumbs to double pané the balls.

Fry the papa rellena, two or three at a time, for
5 minutes, until crisp and golden on the outside
and warm throughout.

WARM SALAD OF ROOT VEG
★
WITH GOATS' CHEESE

Keep the dressing quite sharp here as it cuts well through
the sweetness of roasted veg and the richness of the cheese.
If you want to keep it vegan, switch the honey
for maple syrup and omit the goats' cheese.

SERVES 4

TAKES 50 minutes

350g (12oz) new potatoes,
   scrubbed and chopped into
   large chunks
1 beetroot (beet), peeled and
   chopped into large dice
1 parsnip, peeled and chopped
   into large chunks
1 carrot, peeled and chopped into
   large chunks (or 175g/6oz baby
   carrots, halved lengthways)
2 tbsp olive oil
½ tsp dried thyme
1 apple, cored and chopped
   into wedges
60g (2oz) walnut halves
a drizzle of honey
100g (3½oz) salad leaves
125g (4½oz) soft, crumbly
   goats' cheese
sea salt and freshly ground
   black pepper

Preheat the oven to 180°C/350°F/gas 4.

Put the potatoes and other root veg in a large
roasting pan, drizzle over the olive oil, sprinkle
over the thyme, and season with salt and black
pepper. Toss everything together until all the veg
are well coated. Roast in the preheated oven for
about 20 minutes, or until starting to brown.

Add the apple slices and mix to coat in the thymey
oil. Return the pan to the oven and cook for about
another 15 minutes until all of the veg and the
apple are tender.

Put the walnuts in a small bowl and drizzle over
a little honey. Stir around so that the nuts are well
coated. Sprinkle the walnuts over the veg in the
pan and return to the oven for 5 minutes until the
nuts are toasted and golden.

★ ★

WARM SALAD OF ROOT VEG WITH GOATS' CHEESE

continued...

For the dressing:
1 tbsp walnut oil
1 tbsp olive oil
1 tbsp apple cider vinegar
1 teaspoon Dijon mustard
1 teaspoon honey

Meanwhile, mix together all of the ingredients for the dressing and season well with salt and pepper. Pour half over the salad leaves and toss to coat.

Arrange a bed of salad leaves on a platter and dot the roasted veg and walnuts over the top. Crumble on the goats' cheese and serve with the rest of the dressing drizzled over the top.

INDIAN SWEET POTATO
★
& RED LENTIL SOUP

Basically a blended sweet potato dahl, packed with spices and herbs, this is a supremely comforting and satisfying soup – perfect for wintery days.

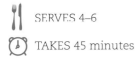 SERVES 4–6

TAKES 45 minutes

1½ tsp coriander seeds
1½ tsp cumin seeds
1½ tsp black mustard seeds
2 tbsp oil
1 onion, diced
3 garlic cloves, finely chopped
1½ tsp ground turmeric
500g (1lb 2oz) sweet potatoes,
    peeled and diced
100g (3½oz/½ cup) dried red lentils
800ml–1 litre (28–35fl oz) hot
    vegetable stock
a squeeze of lemon juice
a small bunch fresh coriander
    (cilantro), chopped
sea salt and freshly ground
    black pepper

Put the spice seeds in a large saucepan and heat gently over a low heat until they start to pop and smell aromatic.

Add the oil and onion and cook for 5 minutes, then add the garlic and turmeric and cook for 5 more minutes. Add in the potatoes and lentils and stir to coat in the spiced oil.

Add 800ml (28fl oz) of the stock and bring the liquid to a boil. Cover and cook for 20–25 minutes, until the potatoes are very tender and the lentils have completely broken down and are thickening the soup.

Transfer the soup to a blender and blend until smooth. If it's too thick, add the remaining stock bit by bit until it reaches the desired consistency. Return the soup to the pan and heat gently to rewarm. Taste and season with salt, pepper and a good squeeze of lemon juice. Stir in most of the coriander, then serve with the rest sprinkled over the top.

CHEESY POTATO
★
TOASTIE

Golden fried potatoes, strings of melted cheese, and a punchy, flavourful chutney, all wrapped up in toasted sourdough; beat that for a lunch.

SERVES 1 (but can be easily scaled up)

TAKES 25 minutes

1 tbsp butter
2 tsp olive oil
100g (3½oz) new potatoes, sliced 3mm (⅛in) thick
2 slices good crusty bread, preferably sourdough
2–3 slices Monterey jack cheese
1–2 tbsp chutney of your choice

In a large non-stick frying pan, melt the butter with the oil. Add the potato slices to the pan and spread out in a single layer. Cook over a medium–low heat for about 10 minutes, until tender and golden, turning them over halfway through cooking.

Preheat a ridged griddle pan over a medium heat.

Lay one of your bread slices out on a large piece of baking parchment. Arrange the potato slices over the bread in an even layer. Lay the cheese slices on top, then smear over the chutney – as much as you want. Place the other slice of bread on top. Wrap the sandwich up in the paper and cut off most of the excess paper at the ends, scrunching up the last little bit so it's out the way of the pan.

Place the sandwich in the pan and place something heavy on top, such as a cast-iron frying pan. Cook for about 4 minutes, then turn the sandwich over and cook on the other side for 4 minutes, again, weighted down. The paper can get a little scorched at the ends, so stay close in case it starts to smoke, and remove from the heat immediately if so. Sneak a peek: if the bread is golden with griddle marks appearing and the cheese is melted, it is ready.

Slice the sandwich in half, still in the paper, and serve.

SESAME SWEET POTATO ★
FALAFEL WRAPS

Sweetly spiced falafel, punchy garlic sauce, and a kick of chilli... finish it off with some lovely, charred Middle Eastern bread and you've got a pretty cracking lunch.

🍴 SERVES 4

⏰ TAKES 30 minutes

2 large sweet potatoes (about 700g/1lb 8oz total weight)
1 tsp ground cumin
1 tsp ground coriander
good pinch of ground cinnamon
3 tbsp finely chopped parsley
1 tbsp finely chopped mint
1½ tsp flaky sea salt
1–3 tbsp gram (chickpea) flour
100g (3½oz/¾ cup) sesame seeds
sunflower oil, for frying
freshly ground black pepper

For the garlic sauce:
150ml (5fl oz/scant ⅔ cup)
    natural yogurt
2 cloves garlic, crushed

To serve:
½ red onion, finely sliced
juice of ½ lemon
4 Middle Eastern flatbreads
lettuce
sliced green chillies

Put the red onion in a small bowl and pour over the lemon juice. Leave to pickle. Combine the yogurt and garlic for the sauce, season and set aside.

Pierce the potatoes a few times with a fork and microwave them for 10–12 minutes until soft and tender throughout. Scoop out the flesh into a large bowl and mash well with a potato masher. Add the spices, herbs, salt and 1 tablespoon of the gram flour and mix in to create a soft dough. Season with salt and pepper. You need a mixture that's firm enough to shape, so add more flour if needs be, but try to add as little as possible. Instead, a little flour on your hands will make them easier to shape.

Divide the mixture roughly into 16 portions and shape them into small patties about 1.5cm (⅔in) thick. Roll them in sesame seeds to coat fully.

Pour oil to the depth of about 1cm (½in) deep in a non-stick frying pan. Fry the falafels, 8 at a time, for a couple of minutes on each side, until the seeds are golden and crispy and the falafels are hot throughout. Place them on kitchen paper to drain.

To assemble your wrap, lay out the breads and top each with lettuce. Add 4 falafels to each one and drizzle over the garlic sauce. Sprinkle over pickled red onions and green chillies, wrap up and enjoy!

COLCANNON & HAM
★
STUFFED JACKETS

The traditional way to serve colcannon is topped with a generous blob of butter that melts over the top, you know, as if the recipe seemed just that bit too healthy. Skip the ham to make it vegetarian.

SERVES 4

TAKES 1½ hours

4 large baking potatoes
30g (1oz/2 tbsp) butter, plus extra
   to serve (optional)
1 tbsp olive oil
½ savoy cabbage, finely shredded
bunch of spring onions (scallions),
   finely sliced
80ml (2½fl oz/⅓ cup) single
   (light) cream
4 thick slices smoked ham, cut
   into thin strips
a grating of nutmeg
sea salt and freshly ground
   black pepper

Preheat the oven to 180ºC/350ºF/gas 4 and pop the potatoes in the oven. Bake for 1–1½ hours, or until the skins are really crisp and the insides totally soft.

Meanwhile, prepare the filling. Melt the butter with the oil in a large frying pan. Add the cabbage and the spring onions (scallions), reserving a little of the spring onion greens to garnish. Fry until just beginning to turn brown.

Once the potatoes are cooked, remove them from the oven and slice them in half. Use a spoon to scrape out the flesh (try not to tear the skins) and spoon it straight into the pan with the cabbage. Pour in the cream and use a potato masher to roughly mash everything together until you have a shaggy, green potatoey mess. Add the sliced ham and stir in, then season with the grated nutmeg, salt and pepper to taste.

Spoon the mixture back into the potato skins, dividing it evenly between them. Top each one with a small blob of butter, if liked, and sprinkle with the reserved spring onion greens to serve.

MAJORCAN

★

TOMBET

This is a classic dish from the island of Majorca, best made in the summer when tomatoes are sweet and ripe, and you can better imagine you're on a Mediterranean terrace.

 SERVES 4

TAKES 50 minutes

3 tbsp olive oil, plus extra for
   drizzling
400g (14oz) waxy potatoes,
   such as Charlotte, sliced
   3mm (⅛in) thick
1 large aubergine (eggplant), sliced
   3–4mm (⅛in) thick
3 jarred roasted red (bell) peppers
   (preserved in oil, not vinegar),
   drained and halved

For the tomato sauce:
2 tbsp olive oil
1 small onion, finely diced
2 large cloves garlic, crushed
4 large ripe tomatoes (about
   800g/1lb 12oz total weight),
   deseeded and diced
a handful of basil leaves, plus
   extra to serve
a pinch of sugar
sea salt and freshly ground
   black pepper

For the sauce, put the oil in a saucepan over a low–medium heat and cook the onion and garlic for 10 minutes, until softened. Add the tomatoes and cook for another 15 minutes or so until everything has broken down. Add the basil leaves and let them wilt into the sauce, then stick an immersion blender in the pan and blitz to a smooth sauce. Taste and season with a pinch of sugar and salt and pepper.

While the sauce is cooking, heat the oil in a large non-stick sauté pan with a lid and cook the potato slices for about 10 minutes, covered with the lid, shaking the pan and turning on occasion, until softened and beginning to pick up some colour.

Meanwhile, drizzle a little oil into a ridged griddle pan and griddle the slices of aubergine (eggplant) over high heat for a few minutes on each side, until softened and showing char lines. You will need to do this in batches, adding more oil as required.

Get yourself a baking dish measuring about 20cm (8in) square and begin to layer up your veg. Start with the aubergine, then the peppers, with the potatoes on top. Finally, spoon the sauce roughly over the top. Pop the dish in the oven and bake for 20 minutes until everything is hot and bubbling, and serve with a few more basil leaves scattered over the top.

POTATO, SALMON &
★
WATERCRESS TART

The flavours in this lovely tart – nutty new pots, peppery
watercress and deeply smoky salmon – are completely
complementary and make a lovely summery lunch with
a glass of something cold.

SERVES 4–6

TAKES 1 hour, plus chilling

375g (13oz) pack ready-rolled
shortcrust pastry
plain (all-purpose) flour, for
dusting
250g (9oz) baby new potatoes,
halved or quartered if large
30g (1oz/2 tbsp) butter
1 tbsp olive oil
small bunch of spring onions
(scallions), finely sliced
85g (3oz) watercress
3 eggs
125ml (4fl oz/½ cup) double
(heavy) cream
200g (7oz) hot smoked salmon
sea salt and freshly ground
black pepper

Roll out the pastry on a flour-dusted surface so
that it will cover the base and sides of a 23cm (9in)
tart tin (pan) generously. Use it to line the tin, and
trim off the excess with a sharp knife leaving a
bit of overhang. Prick the base of the case with a
fork and chill for 30 minutes. Preheat the oven to
190ºC/375º/gas 5.

Cook the potatoes in boiling, salted water for
about 10 minutes, or until tender but still a minute
or two off being perfectly cooked.

Meanwhile, melt the butter with the oil in a large
sauté pan with a lid. Reserve a little of the sliced
spring onion (scallion) greens to sprinkle over
the top and add the rest to the pan. Soften over
a medium heat for about 3 minutes. Add the
watercress to the pan and stir so it's coated in the
butter. Pop a lid on the pan and let it wilt for just
a minute or so before turning off the heat.

Drain the potatoes, add them to the pan and stir
to coat in the butter, then set aside. Whisk the
eggs, then whisk in the cream and season well;
set this aside, too.

★ ★

POTATO, SALMON & WATERCRESS TART
continued...

Remove the chilled pastry case from the fridge and line it with baking parchment and baking beans. Blind bake for 15 minutes, then remove the paper and beans and return to the oven for 10 minutes until turning golden and crispy. Turn the oven down to 170°C/325°F/gas 3.

Remove the pastry from the oven and carefully roll a rolling pin over the top to trim off the edges.

Spread out the potato, watercress and spring onion in the baked case. Flake the salmon into large chunks and distribute it evenly between the potato mix. Pour in the egg mixture and sprinkle over the reserved spring onion greens and a little coarse ground pepper. Return the tart to the oven for about 20 minutes, or until set and turning light golden on top.

SPANAKOPI-TATO

Adding potato to this classic Greek pie makes it far
more substantial – a meal in your hand and perfect for
picnics, although it's nice served fresh from the oven
with a dressed salad.

 SERVES 6–8

TAKES 1 hour

80g (2¾oz/⅓ cup) butter, melted
400g (14oz) waxy potatoes (such
   as Charlotte), halved
2 tbsp olive oil
1 onion, finely diced
3 large garlic cloves, finely diced
1 tsp ground allspice
600g (1lb 5oz) fresh spinach
1 bunch fresh oregano (20g/⅔oz),
   roughly chopped
1 small bunch dill (20g/⅔oz),
   roughly chopped
400g (14oz) feta cheese
3 eggs, beaten
270g (9½oz) pack filo pastry
sea salt and freshly ground
   black pepper

Preheat the oven to 180ºC/350ºF/gas 4 and grease
a 20 x 28cm (8 x 11in) deep baking tin (pan) with a
little of the butter using a pastry brush.

Put the potatoes in a pan of salted water and
bring to the boil. Boil for 12–15 minutes, or until
tender, then drain and leave to cool and steam
dry in the colander.

While the potatoes are cooking, put the oil in a
large sauté pan and add the onion. Cook for a few
minutes until starting to soften, then add the garlic
and allspice. Cook for a few more minutes, then
remove from the heat and set aside to cool a little.

Wilt the spinach in a bowl in the microwave (you'll
have to do this in batches), leave to drain on paper
towels for a while, then squeeze out as much water
as you can. Stir the spinach into the onion mixture,
then add the chopped herbs, feta and eggs. Season
well with black pepper and a little salt if you need
to (remembering that the feta cheese is very salty).

★ ★

SPANAKOPI-TATO

continued...

Line the bottom of the baking tin with a sheet of filo, letting any excess come up the sides of the tin, and brush it with melted butter. Add another sheet and brush with butter again, then add a third sheet.

Chop the cooked potatoes into 1cm (½in) chunks and sprinkle them evenly over the pastry in the tin. Top with the spinach mixture and spread evenly, then fold over any overhanging pastry so it covers the filling. Layer the remaining sheets of filo on top, brushing each one with melted butter as you go. You can cut off any overhang and use it to make another layer of pastry. Score the top of the pie into portions with a sharp knife.

Bake the pie for 35–40 minutes until golden and crispy on top, and hot throughout.

★
POUTINE

Cheddar is not the deal here. What you need is something creamier, that melts into the gravy a little, but still maintains its integrity. Cheese curds is what you need to look out for, but if not, mozzarella comes a close second.

SERVES 4–6

TAKES 15 minutes,
plus making the chips

300ml (10½fl oz/1¼ cups) good
chicken stock
200ml (7fl oz/scant 1 cup) good
beef stock
2 tbsp cornflour (cornstarch)
15g (½oz/1 tbsp) butter
sea salt and freshly ground black
pepper
2 recipe quantities Chips (see
page 16)
250g (9oz) cheese curds or torn
chunks of mozzarella (not
the watery fresh stuff, but
the grateable pizza stuff)

First make the gravy. Heat the chicken and beef stock in a pan until simmering. In a small bowl, mix the cornflour (cornstarch) with a splash of water and stir until you have a smooth liquid. Pour it into the gravy, along with the butter, and simmer until it thickens to the consistency you desire. Taste and season to your liking, then keep it warm over a very low heat while you prepare the chips, as per page 16.

Put the chips in a large serving bowl and season with salt. Dollop the cheese curds over the top (or sprinkle over the chunks of mozzarella, if using that – you may need a little more salt). Pour over half the gravy and stir once or twice to combine and so that the cheese starts melting into the gravy. Serve with the rest of the gravy on the side.

VADA PAV WITH
★
GREEN COCONUT CHUTNEY

Millions of Mumbaians enjoy vada pav – fried balls of spiced, mashed potato, coated in chickpea batter – for lunch every day. You can't argue with that...

 SERVES 4

TAKES 1 hour

For the potato:
2 tsp mustard seeds
2 tsp coriander seeds
1 tbsp ajwain seeds
2 tbsp ghee or butter
10 fresh curry leaves, very finely shredded
1 tsp ground turmeric
1 green chilli, finely chopped
800g (1lb 12oz) floury potatoes, peeled and diced
sea salt

For the chutney:
60g (2oz) fresh coconut
3 tbsp lime juice
a small bunch of coriander (cilantro)
a small handful of mint leaves, chopped
a splash of water

Put the mustard, coriander and ajwain seeds in a large dry sauté pan (with a lid) and toast over a high heat for a couple of minutes until starting to pop. Tip them into a pestle and mortar and grind them to a powder. Add the butter to the pan and melt, then add the ground spices, curry leaves, turmeric and green chilli. Tip in the potatoes and stir to coat in the spiced oil. Add a splash of water and pop the lid on the pan. Cook until the potatoes are soft and tender – about 20 minutes – adding a little more water if it looks like the mixture is starting to catch, but not letting it get too wet. Once the potato is cooked, mash everything together in the pan until you have a smoothish mixture. Set aside until cool enough to handle.

Meanwhile, make the chutney. Remove any tough brown skin from the coconut and chop it into chunks. Put it in a mini chopper or food processor with the lime juice and blitz until it is a rough purée. Add the coriander and mint and a splash of water to loosen it up, so you can blend until everything is very finely chopped. Taste and season with salt.

★ ★

VADA PAV WITH GREEN COCONUT CHUTNEY

continued...

For the batter:
150g (5½oz/1 heaped cup) gram
   (chickpea) flour, plus extra for
   dusting
½ tsp ground turmeric
¼ tsp baking powder

vegetable oil, for frying
4 white bread rolls

Preheat a deep fat fryer or pan of vegetable oil to 170ºC (325ºF).

Mix the chickpea flour with enough water to get a thick batter. Add the turmeric and baking powder, season well with salt, and mix.

Divide the potato mixture into 4 portions, rolling each one into a ball. Sprinkle some extra flour on a plate, then roll each vada in the flour, then into the batter. Carefully drop them into the oil (you will probably need to cook them two at a time, depending on the size of your pan). Cook for 6–7 minutes, until golden on the outside and warmed all the way through.

To serve, slice open the rolls and spread the base with a good amount of the chutney. Place a fried potato ball in each one. Top with the top of the bread roll and serve.

GADO GADO
★
SALAD

An Indonesian classic with a delicious spicy peanut kick.
You can be a bit flexible with the salad ingredients and
adapt it to whatever you have in the fridge, but the
dressing is a must.

 SERVES 4

TAKES 25 minutes

250g (9oz) small new potatoes,
   halved if large
4 eggs
100g (3½oz) green beans
200g (7oz) firm tofu (smoked is
   lovely), sliced into 1cm (½in)
   thick slices
1 head romaine lettuce, roughly
   chopped
a handful of radishes, finely sliced
½ cucumber, finely sliced
a handful of bean sprouts
a few salted, roasted peanuts,
   roughly chopped, to sprinkle

Put the new potatoes in a pan of boiling water and
bring the water back to the boil. Cook for 10–12
minutes, or until tender when pierced with a knife.
Run the pan under cold water to cool them down
and set aside.

Meanwhile, in another saucepan, boil the eggs for
6 minutes, until hard-boiled but still soft in the
middle, then run under cold water to cool them
down. In another pan, blanch the green beans for
3 minutes, until tender but still crisp, then run
under cold water to cool them down.

Heat a little oil in a frying pan and fry the tofu
slices for a couple of minutes on each side, until
golden brown.

★ ★

GADO GADO SALAD
continued...

For the dressing:
2 red chillies
2.5cm (1in) piece of ginger, peeled
and roughly chopped
1 large garlic clove, roughly
chopped
4 tbsp coconut milk
80g (2¾oz/⅓ cup) crunchy
peanut butter
3 tbsp kicap manis (Indonesian
sweet soy sauce)

Put the chillies, ginger and garlic for the dressing in a mini chopper or food processor, and blitz until roughly chopped. You could add a splash of the coconut milk here if you're struggling to blend such a small amount. Tip it into a bowl and add all the remaining dressing ingredients and stir together well.

Now it's time to assemble. Scatter the lettuce over a platter and top with the potatoes, then the tofu and green beans. Scatter over the radish and cucumber slices, followed by the bean sprouts. Peel the eggs, then slice into halves or quarters and place these on top. Drizzle a little dressing over and serve the rest on the side. Finally, sprinkle over the peanuts to serve.

SNACK

★

POTATOES

PIRI PIRI

★

SOUFFLÉED POTATOES

The egg in these makes the potato filling puff up a little
and become surprisingly light. If you want it milder, cut
down on the piri piri seasoning; for more heat, go for
hot piquante peppers.

SERVES 4

TAKES 1¾ hours

4 large baking potatoes
40g (1½oz/2½ tbsp) butter
1 tbsp piri piri seasoning
8 spring onions (scallions),
    finely sliced
12 small, mild jarred piquante
    peppers (such as Peppadew)
125g (4½oz/1¼ cups) grated
    Cheddar cheese
2 large eggs, well beaten
sea salt and freshly ground
    black pepper

Preheat the oven to 180ºC/350ºF/gas 4. Bake the
potatoes for 1–1½ hours, or until tender throughout
when pierced with a knife.

Remove the potatoes from the oven and turn the
oven up to 200ºC/400ºF/gas 6. Slice the potatoes
in half lengthways. Carefully scoop out the flesh,
being careful not to break the skins, and put it in a
bowl. Put the skins on a baking tray.

Add the butter to the potato flesh and mash until
smooth. Add the piri piri seasoning, spring onions
(scallions), peppers and 50g (1¾oz/½ cup) of the
cheese, season well with salt and pepper and stir
until well mixed. Mix in the beaten eggs until well
combined. Pile the potato mixture back into the
skins and scatter the remaining cheese over the
tops, dividing it evenly between the potatoes.

Return the skins to the oven for 15 minutes or so,
until the potatoes have puffed up and the cheese
on top is melted and golden. Serve immediately.

★

POTATO WEDGES

Basic storecupboard staples can add all kinds of bells and whistles to simple potato wedges. A lump of old Parmesan, and a forage around the spice rack and you've somehow made wedges even more moreish.

 SERVES 4

🕐 TAKES 35 minutes

1kg (2lb 4oz) red-skinned potatoes
  (such as Désirée)
3 tbsp olive oil
60g (2oz/½ cup) finely grated
  Parmesan
2 tbsp dried sage
2 tsp garlic powder
sea salt and freshly ground
  black pepper

Preheat the oven to 190ºC/375ºF/gas 5. Line a baking tray with kitchen foil to avoid you having to scrub off burnt cheese.

Chop the potatoes into 6 or 8 wedges each (depending on the size) and put them in a large bowl. Drizzle them with the oil and toss to coat well. Sprinkle in the Parmesan, sage and garlic powder, a little salt (the Parmesan will be salty) and plenty of black pepper and mix so the potatoes are coated.

Place the potatoes on a baking tray and bake for about 30 minutes, or until golden and crisp.

Serve straight away.

POTATO

★

'SCALLOPS'

Not quite as fancy as the word 'scallop' suggests, but definitely a bit fancier than plain ol' chips. Serve with a piece of plain fish for reverse fish and chips, or with any dips you feel like.

SERVES 4

TAKES 20 minutes

100g (3½oz) plain (all-purpose)
    flour
1 tsp baking powder
½ tsp sea salt, plus extra to serve
500g (1lb 2oz) floury potatoes
vegetable oil, for frying

Sift the flour and baking powder into a large bowl. Add the salt, then gradually add 150ml (5fl oz/scant ⅔ cup) cold water, whisking continuously to get rid of any lumps until you have a smooth batter.

Peel and slice the potatoes into 3–4mm (⅛in) slices. Make sure you don't make the slices thicker than this or they won't cook through before the batter reaches the perfect golden-brown hue.

Heat the oil to 170ºC/325ºF in a large pan or deep fat fryer. Working in batches of 6 or so (depending on the size of your pan), dip the potatoes in the batter, then drop them immediately into the oil. Cook for about 4½ minutes, until a rich golden brown and cooked through.

Remove from the oil with a slotted spoon and leave to drain on paper towels while you cook another batch. Repeat until all the potatoes are cooked (if they're not being snaffled as fast as you cook them, you might want to keep them hot in a warm oven). Sprinkle with sea salt to serve.

UNAUTHENTIC SPANISH ★ CROQUETAS

Croquettes are often confused with real Spanish croquetas, which don't have a potato in sight. But there's rarely a reason to exclude the lovely spud, so these combine potato with all those great Spanish flavours.

MAKES 12

TAKES 45 minutes, plus chilling

For the croquetas:
600g (1lb 5oz) floury potatoes, peeled and chopped into large chunks
4 tbsp olive oil
1 egg yolk
2 tsp sweet smoked paprika
2 tbsp tomato purée (paste)
100g (3½oz) Serrano ham, diced
100g (3½oz) Manchego cheese, diced
sea salt and freshly ground black pepper
mahonesa con ajo (garlic mayo!), to serve

For cooking:
plain (all-purpose) flour, for dusting
2 eggs, beaten
100g (3½oz/1 cup) dried breadcrumbs
sunflower oil, for frying

Put the potatoes in a pan of cold, salted water and bring to the boil. Boil for about 15 minutes, or until tender and a knife can be inserted easily. Drain well, then tip them into a large bowl. Add the olive oil, egg yolk, paprika and tomato purée (paste) and mash them really well until there are no lumps. Stir in the ham and cheese. Season well with salt and pepper.

Divide the mixture into 16 portions and roll each of them into a sausage shape. Put them on a tray and cover with cling film (plastic wrap), then chill in the fridge for 20 minutes or so.

Put the oil in a saucepan and heat it to 180ºC/350ºF.

Put the flour on a plate, the eggs in a shallow bowl and the breadcrumbs on another plate. One at a time, dip the croquetas into the flour, then cover in the egg, then coat completely in breadcrumbs.

Fry the croquetas, a few at a time, in the oil for 3½ minutes, until golden and crispy. Allow to drain on kitchen paper for a few minutes before serving hot with *mahonesa con ajo*.

SMOKY BBQ

★

TORNADOES

Longer, slightly thinner potatoes work best for this. As do wooden skewers, rather than metal, as the texture on them helps grip the potato and hold the spirals open.

 MAKES 8

TAKES 45 minutes

4 tbsp olive oil
2 tbsp maple syrup
1 tbsp sweet smoked paprika
½ tsp garlic powder
1 tsp dried thyme
1 tsp dried ancho chilli flakes
1 tsp smoked sea salt
a good grind of black pepper
8 large waxy potatoes, unpeeled

Preheat the oven to 200ºC/400ºF/gas 6 and line a large baking tray with kitchen foil.

Combine the oil and maple syrup in a small bowl. In another small bowl, combine all the dried seasonings.

Skewer a potato lengthways and place it on a chopping board. Place a knife at one end of the potato and angle it slightly so that the end of blade nearest your hand is pointing into the potato. Slice down until the knife hits the skewer, then turn the potato, keeping the knife always 3mm (⅛in) from the cut edge, so that you are cutting a continuous line through the potato (this may take a bit of practice). Once you have gone all the way through, you should be able to spread the potato out and have one long spiral around the skewer.

Brush the spirals with the oil and maple mixture, then sprinkle over the dry seasoning. Tilt the spirals as you do this so that the seasoning goes in and sticks to the inside of the spiral.

Place the spirals on the prepared baking tray and bake for 30–35 minutes, turning over once or twice for even cooking, until the potato is golden and crisping up. Serve hot.

POTATO & PEA
★
SAMOSAS

Spiced potatoes and peas, all wrapped up in golden fried
pastry, make a perfect snack served with mint raita.

🍴 MAKES 12

⏰ TAKES 50 minutes

30g (1oz/2 tbsp) ghee or butter
1 tbsp vegetable or sunflower oil,
    plus an extra 1 litre (35fl oz/
    4 cups) or so for deep frying
1 onion, finely diced
2 garlic cloves, finely chopped
2.5cm (1in) piece of fresh root
    ginger, finely chopped
300g (10oz) waxy potatoes, peeled
    and cut into 1cm (½in) dice
2 tsp coriander seeds
1 tsp cumin seeds
1 tsp black mustard seeds
1 tsp ajwain seeds
1 tsp ground turmeric
1 tsp garam masala
125g (4½oz/1 cup) frozen peas
small bunch of coriander
    (cilantro), roughly chopped
a squeeze of lemon juice
12 samosa wrappers (measuring
    about 25 x 8cm/10 x 3¼in)
sea salt and freshly ground
    black pepper
mint raita, to serve (optional)

In a large saucepan, melt the butter with the oil
over a low heat and add the onion. Cook for 5
minutes, then add the garlic and ginger and cook
for a minute more, then add the potato and all
the spices. Cook for a few minutes, stirring, until
everything is well coated. Add a splash of water and
pop a lid on the pan. Cook for about 15 minutes,
still over a low heat, until the potatoes are tender.
Watch and add a splash more water if it starts to
stick. Once the potatoes are almost cooked, add
the peas and cook for a couple of minutes, then
remove from the heat and stir in the coriander and
lemon juice. Taste and season with salt and pepper.

Lay out a strip of the samosa pastry with a short
end towards you and spoon about a tablespoon
of the potato mixture into the bottom right
corner. Fold the corner with the filling over, then
keep folding the triangle over, up the length of the
pastry strip, until the triangle is sealed on every
side. Dampen the final bit of pastry with a little
water so that it sticks and seals the samosa.

Heat a pan of oil to 180°C/350°F. Once up to
temperature, cook the samosas, about three at
a time, for 3–4 minutes, or until golden brown.
Remove from the oil with a slotted spoon and drain
on kitchen paper while you cook the next batch.
Serve hot with raita on the side, if using.

RÖSTIS WITH SMOKED SALMON
★
& SOUR CREAM

For a snack, these bite-sized rösti are rather fancy, but
when you're in the mood... It means they make great
canapés too.

MAKES 12

TAKES 45 minutes

25g (¾oz/1½ tbsp) butter, melted,
plus extra for greasing
450g (1lb) good all-rounder
potatoes, about 3 medium
potatoes, unpeeled and left
whole
½ tbsp olive oil
½ onion, finely sliced
½ tsp caraway seeds
1 egg, beaten

For the topping:
100g (3½oz) smoked salmon,
ripped into rough strips
1 tsp creamed horseradish
60ml (2fl oz/¼ cup) sour cream
snipped dill, to sprinkle
sea salt and freshly ground
black pepper

Preheat the oven to 190ºC/375ºF/gas 5 and grease a
shallow 12-hole bun pan with butter.

Put the potatoes in a pan of cold water and bring to
the boil. Cook for about 8 minutes, until starting to
soften, but still quite firm. Drain and leave to cool.

Meanwhile, heat the oil in a large frying pan and
add the onion and caraway seeds. Sauté gently for
10 minutes until the onion is translucent and tender,
but not coloured. Remove from the heat.

Once the potatoes are cool enough to handle,
grate them coarsely on a box grater. Tip them into
the pan with the onion, add the egg and seasoning,
and mix gently until everything is well combined.

Press the mixture into the holes in the bun tin,
dividing it evenly as you go. Brush a little melted
butter over the top of each rösti with a pastry
brush. Pop the tray in the oven and bake for
20 minutes, until golden and crisp at the edges.

Meanwhile, mix the horseradish cream into the
sour cream and set aside.

Let the rösti cool for a few minutes in the tray,
then transfer to a serving plate. Top each with
a teaspoon of sour cream, and curl a ribbon of
salmon on top. Sprinkle with dill and serve.

KOREAN SWEET POTATO &
★
KIMCHI MANDU

Korean sweet potatoes are reddish purple on the outside
and yellow in the middle and make a great filling for these
fried dumplings, paired with punchy Korean pickles.

 MAKES 16

TAKES 30 minutes

600g (1lb 6oz) Korean sweet
    potatoes
150g (5½oz) fresh kimchi,
    roughly chopped
4 spring onions (scallions),
    finely sliced
1½ tsp sesame oil
1 tbsp soy sauce
16 gyoza pastry wrappers
vegetable oil, for deep frying
sea salt

For the dipping sauce:
3 tbsp soy sauce
1 tbsp rice vinegar
2 tsp toasted sesame oil
1 tbsp toasted seasame seeds
½ long red chilli, finely sliced

Cook the sweet potatoes in the microwave for
about 10 minutes until tender. Scoop the flesh
out into a bowl and mash roughly. Add the kimchi,
spring onions (scallions), sesame oil and soy sauce
and season with salt.

Lay a gyoza wrapper out and spoon a couple of
teaspoons of the sweet potato mixture into it,
arranging it in a rough semi-circle over one side
of the pastry and leaving a border clear around the
entire edge. Dampen the edge with a little water
and fold the pastry over to make a half moon,
pressing the edges together to seal. Repeat to use
all the filling – you should be able to make about
16 dumplings.

Heat the oil for deep frying in a large saucepan
to 170ºC/325ºF. Fry the dumplings in batches
for about 4 minutes, until golden and crisp.
Remove from the oil with a strainer and let drain
on kitchen paper.

While you are cooking the dumplings, combine the
ingredients for the dipping sauce in a small bowl.
Serve the dumplings hot with the sauce.

PATATAS

★

BRAVAS

The 'bravas' is the courage to eat as much of the spicy sauce as you can with your potatoes. *Cobardes* can cut down on the crushed chillies, if they must

SERVES 4

TAKES 30 minutes

800g (1lb 12oz) white potatoes, peeled and diced
sunflower or vegetable oil, for deep frying

For the sauce:
2 tbsp olive oil
1 onion, finely diced
2 large garlic cloves, finely chopped
1 x 400g (14oz) can chopped tomatoes
1 tbsp tomato purée (paste)
1 tsp sweet smoked paprika
1–2 tsp crushed chilli (hot pepper) flakes (depending how hot you want it)
1 tsp sugar
sea salt and freshly ground black pepper

Start by making the sauce. Heat the oil in a saucepan and add the onion. Cook for 5 minutes until beginning to soften. Add the garlic and cook for another few minutes, then add the chopped tomatoes. Fill the tomato can one-third full with water, swill it around and add it to the pan. Add the tomato purée (paste), paprika, chilli (hot pepper) flakes and sugar and bring the sauce to a simmer. Let it simmer for about 10 minutes, stirring occasionally, until thickening. Taste and season.

Meanwhile, heat a pan of salted water over a high heat. Once boiling, add the potatoes and parboil for 5 minutes. Drain and let steam dry in a colander.

Heat the oil in a deep saucepan to about 170ºC (325ºF) and deep fry the potatoes in batches for about 4 minutes, until turning golden and crisp on the outside and soft and fluffy inside. Drain on kitchen paper.

Put the potatoes into one large bowl or divide them between smaller tapas dishes. Drizzle a good amount of sauce over the top and serve the rest on the side.

HOT POTATO DOGS WITH
MAPLE ONIONS

These are the cutest little snacks and so easy to make. Using vegetables also feels a bit more saintly than using sweet, white bread rolls for your hot dogs.

MAKES 12

TAKES 50 minutes

12 small white potatoes
  (each about 50g/1¾oz)
1 tbsp olive oil
1 onion, finely sliced
2 tbsp maple syrup
12 cocktail sausages
sea salt and freshly ground
  black pepper
American-style yellow mustard,
  to serve

Preheat the oven to 190°C/375°F/gas 5.

Wash the potatoes and pop them on a baking tray. Bake them in the oven for 40–45 minutes until crisp on the outside and soft and tender in the middle.

Once the potatoes are in, start the onions. Heat the oil in a saucepan over a low heat and add the onion and a pinch of salt. Cook for 10 minutes until starting to really soften, stirring frequently. Add the maple syrup and continue to cook for another 5–10 minutes until meltingly tender and caramelizing. Season with salt and pepper and set aside.

Pop the sausages onto a baking tray and add them to the oven, on the shelf above the potatoes, for the last 25 minutes of the potatoes' cooking time.

Once everything is cooked, it's time to assemble. Slice each potato down the middle lengthways. Add a spoonful of the onions to the potato, then add a sausage. Squirt mustard along the sausage and serve.

SPANISH
★
TORTILLA

A true Spanish staple, this makes a great (healthyish) snack, or can be served as a small plate alongside other tapas treats, such as the Patatas Bravas on page 96.

SERVES 4

TAKES 1 hour

30g (1oz/2 tbsp) butter
3 tbsp olive oil
2 onions (or 1 very large), finely
  sliced
400g (14oz) waxy new potatoes
  (such as Charlotte), sliced 3mm
  (⅛in) thick
6 large eggs, beaten
sea salt and freshly ground
  black pepper

Melt the butter with the oil in a non-stick 23cm (9in) frying pan over a medium–low heat. Add the onions and cook for 10 minutes until really softening.

Add the potatoes and stir to coat in the oil, then pop the lid on and cook for another 20 minutes or so until tender. Stir occasionally to make sure the potatoes cook evenly, but don't mash them about too much once they really start to soften as you don't want them to all break up.

Season the beaten eggs well with salt and pepper. Once the potatoes are tender, remove the pan lid and pour the eggs over the potatoes and onion and put the pan lid back on. Cook, still over a low–medium heat, for 20 minutes, until golden underneath and starting to set on top.

Place a plate on the top of the pan and carefully (wearing oven gloves) invert the pan so the tortilla falls onto the plate, cooked side up. Slide the tortilla back into the frying pan and continue to cook for another 5 minutes or so until browned on the other side and cooked through.

Slice into wedges and serve.

SIDE

★

POTATOES

SIMPLE SALT 'N' PEPPER
★
HASSELBACKS

These are a lot easier to achieve than you might think. The skewer is your friend here, stopping you cutting all the way through so you can achieve lots of delicate, thin slices to trap all that lovely seasoning.

 SERVES 4

TAKES 1 hour

800g (1lb 12oz) waxy potatoes, such as Charlotte (all of an even size, and longer ones are good here)
2 tbsp olive oil
sea salt and freshly ground black pepper

Preheat the oven to 190°C/375°F/gas 5.

Insert a metal skewer into a potato lengthways, about 5mm (¼in) in from one side. Place the potato, skewer side down, onto a chopping board. Starting at one end and working along the length of the potato, make incisions with a sharp knife about 3mm (⅛in) apart, cutting down each time until the knife hits the skewer. This will stop you cutting all the way through and the potato breaking up. Once you have reached the other end of the potato, remove the skewer, place the potato on the baking tray, and repeat until all the potatoes are sliced in the same way.

Drizzle the potatoes with the oil and sprinkle plenty of salt and pepper over each one. Bake the potatoes for 40–50 minutes until golden brown and tender and the slits have opened up.

CHICKENY
★
POTATO BALLS

Don't be too aghast at the wastage here – you can always
boil up the potato scraps and use them for mash or in any
of the other recipes that need mashed potatoes. And half
the enjoyment of these is the perfect little balls.

 SERVES 4

TAKES 30 minutes

1kg (2lb 4oz) white potatoes,
    peeled
60g (2oz/4 tbsp) butter
1 chicken jelly stock pot
1 tbsp finely chopped parsley
sea salt

Using a melon baller, make as many little balls of
potato as you can from the potatoes. Put them in
a bowl of water as you go to stop them browning.

Get a large pan of salted water boiling. Drain the
potato balls, add them to the pan and blanch them
for 4 minutes, then drain and leave them to steam
dry in the colander.

Melt the butter in a large non-stick sauté pan with
a lid over a medium–high heat. Add the potato
balls and pop the lid on. Cook for 5 minutes,
shaking the pan occasionally so they are beginning
to pick up some colour. Remove the lid and
cook for 5 more minutes, turning up the heat if
necessary, or until they have really browned off
and are a lovely golden colour.

Carefully drain off any excess butter in the pan.
Push the potatoes to one side of the pan and add
the jelly stock to the other. Once it has melted
from the heat of the pan, stir it into the potatoes.
Cook for a few more minutes until they are dried
and crisp again. Taste and season with salt, then stir
in the parsley just before serving.

POTATO, CELERIAC & BLUE CHEESE
★
DAUPHINOISE

While we love a spud, adding a bit of celeriac to this
dauphinoise gives it a bit of a twist on the classic flavour,
not to mention all that lovely blue cheese. A mandoline will
make this recipe a lot quicker to get in the oven.

SERVES 4–6

TAKES 1½ hours

700g (1lb 8oz) Désirée (or other
  floury) potatoes, peeled and
  sliced 3mm (⅛in) thick
½ celeriac (celery root), peeled
  and sliced 3mm (⅛in) thick
300ml (10½fl oz/1¼ cups) double
  (heavy) cream
200ml (7fl oz/scant 1 cup)
  whole milk
1 garlic clove, bashed
150g (5½oz) blue cheese, such
  as Stilton
sea salt and freshly ground
  black pepper

Preheat the oven to 180ºC/350ºF/gas 4.

Put the milk, cream and garlic in a large saucepan
or sauté pan and bring to a simmer. Add the potato
and celeriac (celery root) slices and stir so that they
are all coated in the liquid. Put a lid on and simmer
for 6 minutes or so, gently stirring occasionally,
until the vegetables are beginning to soften, but
still reasonably firm.

Using a slotted spoon, scoop out about one-third
of the potato and celeriac and arrange in a layer
over the base of a large, greased baking dish. When
you come across the bashed garlic clove, remove
and discard it. Crumble over half of the blue
cheese. Add another layer of potato and celeriac
and then another layer of cheese. Finish with the
final one-third of the vegetables.

Pour the creamy mixture from the pan over the
top of the dish. Put the dauphinoise in the oven
and bake for about 1 hour, or until the vegetables
feel tender when a knife is inserted and it is golden
on top. Check it during cooking and cover the dish
loosely with kitchen foil if it looks like it is getting
too brown. Serve hot.

SAFFRON

★

BOULANGÈRE

Saffron adds not only a lovely colour, but also a subtle flavour twist to this French classic. Use the best stock you can find – splash out on a fresh pot or pouch – as it's the basis for the flavour.

 SERVES 4–6

TAKES 1¼ hours

a good pinch of saffron threads
300ml (10½fl oz/1¼ cups) really good, flavoursome chicken stock (or use vegetable if you need to), warmed
1kg (2lb 4oz) floury potatoes (such as Maris Piper), peeled
50g (1¾oz/3½ tbsp) butter, plus extra for greasing
½ onion, sliced wafer thin (preferably on a mandoline)
sea salt and freshly ground black pepper

Preheat the oven to 180°C/350°F/gas 4.

Add the saffron to the warm stock and leave to infuse while you start layering up.

Slice the potatoes into 3–4mm (⅛in) thick slices, ideally using a mandoline. Put a layer of potatoes over the bottom of a greased 1.5 litre (52fl oz) baking dish and sprinkle over half of the onion slices. Add a few tiny knobs of butter (not more than 10g/⅓oz or so) and grind over a bit of seasoning, then pour over a little of the saffron stock.

Add another layer of potato, the remaining onions, a few more little blobs of butter and more seasoning, then pour over more stock.

Add the final layer of potatoes and the remaining stock. Blob over the final butter and pop the dish in the oven. Bake for 1 hour until golden on top and the potatoes are cooked through.

SWEET POTATO

★

CASSEROLE WITH PECANS

This is a real crowd-pleaser, especially with the kids. Pecans
add an extra crunch and a wonderfully nutty flavour.

SERVES 6

TAKES 45 minutes

80g (2¾oz/⅓ cup) butter, melted
1 tsp ground cinnamon
½ tsp ground ginger
1 tsp flaky sea salt
1.5kg (3lb 5oz) sweet potatoes,
    peeled and diced
75g (2½oz/⅔ cup) pecans
150g (5½oz/scant 4 cups) mini
    marshmallows

Combine the butter with the spices and salt in a
small bowl.

Preheat the oven to 180ºC/350ºF/gas 4. Put the
sweet potato dice into a 23cm (9in) square baking
dish. Pour the spiced butter over and stir so all the
potato is well coated. Cover the tray with foil and
place in the oven for 25–30 minutes, until the sweet
potato is soft and tender, stirring halfway through.

While the potato is cooking, put the pecans on
another baking tray and toast in the oven for 6–7
minutes, until smelling lovely and toasty. Let them
cool a little, then roughly chop.

Once the potato is cooked, take the baking dish
out of the oven and switch the oven to grill (or you
can use a chef's blowtorch for the next bit).

Stir the potatoes again, mashing them a little as you
go, but leaving the mixture quite lumpy with a good
amount of texture. Stir in the pecans, then level
the mixture, tip the marshmallows over the top
and spread them level too.

Put the dish back under the grill to toast the
marshmallows, or use a blowtorch to slightly melt
and brown the marshmallows before serving.

POTATO & CAULIFLOWER
★
PURÉE

A bit old school? Well, maybe. But it's so versatile and can be personalized to whatever you are serving. With a piece of meat, a grating of nutmeg is lovely. With fish, skip the nutmeg and stir in lemon zest and finely chopped parsley.

SERVES 4–6

TAKES 25 minutes

400g (14oz) floury potatoes, peeled
  and cut into chunks
600g (1lb 5oz) cauliflower florets
  (about 1 medium cauliflower)
150ml (5fl oz/scant ⅔ cup) double
  (heavy) cream
40g (1½oz/2½ tbsp) butter
a good grating of nutmeg
  (optional)
sea salt flakes

Put the potatoes in cold water and bring to the boil, then boil for 20 minutes, or until very tender.

Meanwhile, get another pan of water boiling, then add the cauliflower. Cook for 6–7 minutes until completely tender.

Once the potatoes are cooked, drain and mash them roughly.

Put the cauliflower in a food processor with the cream and butter and blitz until as smooth as possible. Add the potatoes, seasoning and a good grating of nutmeg and blitz briefly to combine (don't blend for too long once the potatoes are in). Taste and adjust the seasoning and serve immediately.

GARLIC BUTTERED
★
SMASHED POTATOES

The flatter these go, the crispier they get, so potato mashers
at the ready. But how garlicky can you go?

 SERVES 4

TAKES 45 minutes

1kg (2lb 4oz) small white potatoes
   (all of an even size)
80g (2¾oz/⅓ cup) butter
2 tbsp olive oil
4 large garlic cloves (or more or
   less to taste), crushed
sea salt flakes
mayo, or condiment(s) of your
   choice, to serve

Put the whole, unpeeled potatoes in a pan of
cold, salted water and bring to the boil. Cook for
25 minutes or so, or until really tender. Meanwhile,
preheat the oven to 200ºC/400ºF/gas 6.

Melt the butter in a small pan or in a bowl in the
microwave and stir in the olive oil and garlic.

Once the potatoes are cooked, drain them and
leave them in the colander to steam dry for a few
minutes. Transfer them to a large baking tray and,
using a potato masher, crush the potatoes until
they are flattened and bursting, but you still want
them all in one piece, so don't go too far.

Spoon a generous spoonful of the garlic butter
over each potato, then sprinkle them with salt
flakes. Put the tray in the oven and bake for about
20 minutes, or until golden and crispy.

Serve the potatoes hot with mayo, or with the
sauce of your choice.

POTATOES WITH HERB,
★
LEMON & CAPER BUTTER

You can double up on the butter here and keep the other half in the freezer, wrapped in a parchment roll, salami-style, and just cut off a slice or two whenever you need it. This makes a perfect side for fish.

SERVES 4

TAKES 20 minutes

800g (1lb 12oz) baby new potatoes, halved
100g (3½oz/7 tbsp) butter, softened
2 tbsp freshly squeezed lemon juice
zest of 1 lemon
15g (½oz) tarragon, roughly chopped
15g (½oz) parsley, roughly chopped
15g (½oz) dill, roughly chopped
2 tbsp baby capers, roughly chopped
sea salt and freshly ground black pepper

Put the potatoes in a pan of cold, salted water and bring to the boil. Once boiling, boil for about 10–12 minutes, or until the potatoes are tender throughout when pierced with a knife.

While the potatoes are cooking, put the butter in a mixing bowl, add the lemon juice and beat with a spoon to loosen it. Add the lemon zest, all the herbs and the capers and mix in. Season with salt and plenty of black pepper and leave to one side.

Once the potatoes are cooked, drain them in a colander, then tip them back into the hot pan. Scoop the herb butter into the pan and mix until the butter melts completely and coats the potatoes.

DUCHESS
★
POTATOES

The fanciness of these belies their simplicity. They are basically mash piped into a pretty shape, but with the added benefit of the lovely golden crispy bottoms.

SERVES 6

TAKES 50 minutes

800g (1lb 12oz) floury potatoes, peeled and chopped into large chunks
45g (1½oz/3 tbsp) butter, plus extra melted butter for brushing
3 tbsp double (heavy) cream
3 egg yolks
a good pinch of ground nutmeg
sea salt and freshly ground black pepper

Put the potatoes in a pan of cold, salted water and bring to the boil. Boil for 15–18 minutes, or until tender and a knife can be inserted easily. Drain well, then tip them into a large bowl. Add the butter and mash them really well until there are no lumps. Mash in the cream and egg yolks, then season well with salt and pepper and a good pinch of nutmeg.

Meanwhile, preheat the oven to 220°C/425°F/gas 7 and line 2 baking sheets with baking parchment.

Put the mash in a piping bag fitted with a large star nozzle (tip). Pipe little piles of the potato onto the baking sheets. Pop them in the oven for 10 minutes. Once the outside of the potatoes has firmed up a little, remove them from the oven and brush them with melted butter, being careful not to flatten all those lovely ridges that will crisp up. Return them to the oven and bake for another 10 minutes or so until golden brown all over.

SCOTTISH

★

CLAPSHOT

There is a bit of confusion here over the veg involved, as while the classic recipe calls for turnips, it is actually swede that is included with the potatoes, which the Scottish called turnips. Clear as mud?

 SERVES 4

TAKES 30 minutes

500g (1lb 2oz), floury potatoes, peeled and diced
1 swede (rutabaga) (about 500g/ 1lb 2oz), peeled and diced
45g (1½oz/3 tbsp) butter
1 small onion, diced
a splash of milk, if needed
sea salt and freshly ground black pepper
1 tbsp snipped chives, to serve

Put the potatoes in a pan of salted water and bring to the boil. Once boiling, cook for about 15 minutes, or until tender throughout.

Do the same with the swede (rutabaga), putting it in a different pan as it will probably cook slightly slower than the potatoes. Cook for about 20 minutes, or until tender.

Meanwhile, melt the butter in a large saucepan over a low heat and cook the onion gently for at least 10 minutes, until translucent and tender.

Once the potatoes and swede are cooked, drain them and leave to steam dry in the colander for a few minutes (they can go in together, that's fine). Tip the root veg into the pan, add the butter and onion, and mash well with a potato masher. Add a splash of milk, if needed, to loosen and season well with salt and pepper.

Make sure everything is well stirred together and the onion is distributed evenly throughout the mixture, then tip into a serving dish. Sprinkle with the snipped chives to serve.

SAG

★

ALOO

This is a lighter-flavoured version of the Indian classic, with coconut oil adding a delicate underlying flavour and a real freshness from the hit of herbs and lemon.

SERVES 4

TAKES 25 minutes

800g (1lb 12oz) potatoes, peeled and cut into 2.5cm (1in) cubes
1½ tsp black mustard seeds
1½ tsp cumin seeds
2 tbsp coconut oil
1 onion, finely sliced
2.5cm (1in) piece fresh ginger, peeled and sliced into thin matchsticks
4 garlic cloves, finely sliced
2 green chillies, deseeded and finely sliced (leave the seeds in if you want it hotter)
1 tsp ground turmeric
250ml (9fl oz/1 cup) vegetable stock
250g (9oz) spinach leaves
30g (1oz) coriander (cilantro), chopped (stalks and all)
a good squeeze of lemon juice
sea salt

Put the potatoes in a pan of boiling, salted water and parboil for 6 minutes. Drain and let them steam dry in the colander.

Meanwhile, heat a non-stick sauté pan over medium heat, add the mustard and cumin seeds and cook until you can hear them start to pop. Add the coconut oil and let it melt, then add the onion and cook for 5 minutes. Stir in the ginger, garlic, chilli and turmeric and cook for a minute or so further.

Add the parboiled potato and stock to the pan and pop the lid on. Cook, stirring regularly, for about 10–12 minutes or until the potato is cooked through.

Add the spinach to the pan, put the lid back on and let it wilt in the heat of the pan. You may need to add half, wait for it to wilt down a little, then add the other half if you can't fit it all in the pan at once.

Once the spinach is all wilted, stir in the lemon juice and coriander and season well with salt.

SWEDISH

★

DILL & POTATO STEW

This isn't so much a stew as a lovely, herby potato side dish, despite the name. But throw in the traditional sausage or meatball accompaniment and you have the base for a satisfying, Scandi-style meal.

🍴 SERVES 4

⏰ TAKES 25 minutes

800g (1lb 12oz) floury potatoes, peeled and cut into large dice
30g (1oz/2 tbsp) butter
2 tbsp plain (all-purpose) flour
250ml (9fl oz/1 cup) whole milk
50ml (1¾fl oz/3½ tbsp) double (heavy) cream
a large bunch of dill, chopped
sea salt and freshly ground black pepper

Put the potatoes in a pan of salted water and bring to the boil. Boil for 15–20 minutes, or until tender, then drain and leave to cool and steam dry in the colander.

Meanwhile, melt the butter in a large saucepan over low–medium heat. Add the flour and cook gently for a good 5 minutes, stirring, to cook off the flavour of the flour.

Add a dash of the milk to the pan and whisk in until you have a smooth mixture. Add a little more and do the same, repeating to gradually add all of the milk. Whisk well so that there are no lumps. Cook the sauce for another 5 minutes or so, until thickened and you can't taste the flour when you try it, then stir in the potatoes.

Add the cream and stir through, heating for a minute or so more, then season well with salt and black pepper. Just before serving, stir through all of the chopped dill.

DUTCH 'HOT LIGHTNING'
★
POTATO & APPLE STEW

It sounds like an odd combo, but this Dutch stew is a perfect side for pork of any kind. The key to it is plenty of black pepper to give it a real kick.

SERVES 4

TAKES 35 minutes

800g (1lb 12oz) floury potatoes, peeled and chopped into large dice
600g (1lb 5oz) sour apples (such as Bramley), peeled, cored and chopped into large chunks (twice the size of the potatoes)
400g (14oz) sweet eating apples (such as Golden Delicious), peeled, cored and chopped into eighths
400ml (14fl oz/1¾ cups) hot beef stock
45g (1½oz/3 tbsp) butter
sea salt and freshly ground black pepper

Put the potatoes in the bottom of a large pan with a lid. Sprinkle the diced sour apples over the potatoes, and finally, top with the sweet apples. Pour in the stock – it should cover the potatoes, but doesn't need to cover all the apples as they will cook more gently in the steam. Pop the lid on a bring the mixture to a simmer. Then cook for 20–25 minutes over a low–medium heat, until the potatoes and both types of apple are tender when pierced with a knife. Keep an eye on it as you don't want the apples reducing down to apple sauce.

Add the butter and season with salt and plenty of black pepper. Mash the mixture slightly, but make sure you leave plenty of texture, and even a few big lumps. Taste and adjust the seasoning as needed before serving.

POTATO

★

GALETTES

These make a really pretty base for a fancy meal. Just top with whatever you wish – a piece of meat, fish or veggie option. Get red-skinned potatoes and you will have lovely little potato flowers with pink-tinted edges to the petals.

SERVES 4

TAKES 40 minutes

500g (1lb 2oz) red-skinned potatoes (such as Désirée)
40g (1½oz/2½ tbsp) butter, melted
leaves stripped from a few stalks of fresh thyme (optional)
sea salt

Preheat oven to 180ºC/350ºF/gas 4 and use a pastry brush to well grease a heavy baking tray.

Wash the potatoes well, but don't peel them, then slice them on a mandoline to about 3mm (⅛in) thick. Put them in a large bowl and drizzle over most of the butter. Gently stir the butter, some salt, and the thyme leaves, if using, through the potato so the slices are well coated, being careful not to break them up.

Start layering up the potatoes on the greased tray. Arrange the potato slices in circles, to make 4 rounds, each about 15cm (6in) across. Keep layering up on top to make the galettes thicker, until you have used all the potatoes. Use the reserved butter to brush generously over the top of the galettes.

Place a layer of greaseproof paper over the galettes, then place a second heavy baking tray on top of the first, squashing down the galettes. Bake for 25–30 minutes, removing the top tray for the last 5 minutes or so to get them golden and crisp on top. Use a fish slice or spatula to prise them from the tray and serve topped with whatever you wish.

STRAW

★

POTATOES

If it's possible, these are even more moreish than normal chips or fries – and also make 'chips' acceptable alongside a much fancier meal. If you don't have a mandoline, be prepared for a good 15 minutes of practising your knife skills.

 SERVES 4

TAKES 30 minutes

600g (1lb 5oz) floury potatoes, peeled
vegetable oil, for frying
sea salt

Slice the potatoes into matchsticks, transferring them to a bowl of water as you go. This will help get rid of some of the starch and stop them from going brown too. Once done, drain in a colander and rinse for a while under running water to remove more of the starch. Once soaked and rinsed, dry them as well as you can with kitchen paper or a clean tea towel. These can be quite wet as they have a lot of surface area, and will spit like crazy when they go in the fryer if they aren't dried really well.

Heat the oil to 190ºC/375ºF in a large saucepan with a thermometer or a deep fat fryer. Cook the potatoes in batches for about 3 minutes, until golden and crisp. Drain on kitchen paper while you cook the next batch.

Season well with salt before serving.

MAIN

★

POTATOES

POTATO, GORGONZOLA, ROSEMARY
★
& FIG PIZZAS

The toppings here make an intriguing change from what some would consider obligatory pizza fare, and the flavour is a world away from your average Margarita. This recipe makes two large pizzas.

SERVES 4

TAKES 1 hour, plus proving the dough

For the pizza dough:
450g (1lb/3¼ cups) strong white bread flour, plus extra for dusting
1 x 7g (¼oz) sachet dried yeast
250ml (9fl oz/1 cup) luke-warm water
2 tbsp olive oil, plus extra for greasing
1 tsp fine sea salt

To make the pizza dough, put the flour in the bowl of a stand mixer and make a well in the centre. Add all the remaining ingredients and knead with a dough hook for about 10 minutes, or until the dough is smooth and stretchy. Transfer the dough to a greased bowl, cover with cling film (plastic wrap) and leave to rise in a warm place for about 45 minutes, or until doubled in size.

Knock the air out of the dough and divide it into two smooth balls. Place on a greased tray and cover again with greased cling film and leave for another 30 minutes or so, until risen again. Meanwhile, preheat the oven to 240ºC/475ºF/gas 8 and put a pizza stone or heavy baking tray in the oven to heat up.

To make the topping, boil the potatoes in salted water until almost tender – about 1 minute off being perfectly cooked, then drain and leave to cool a little in the colander.

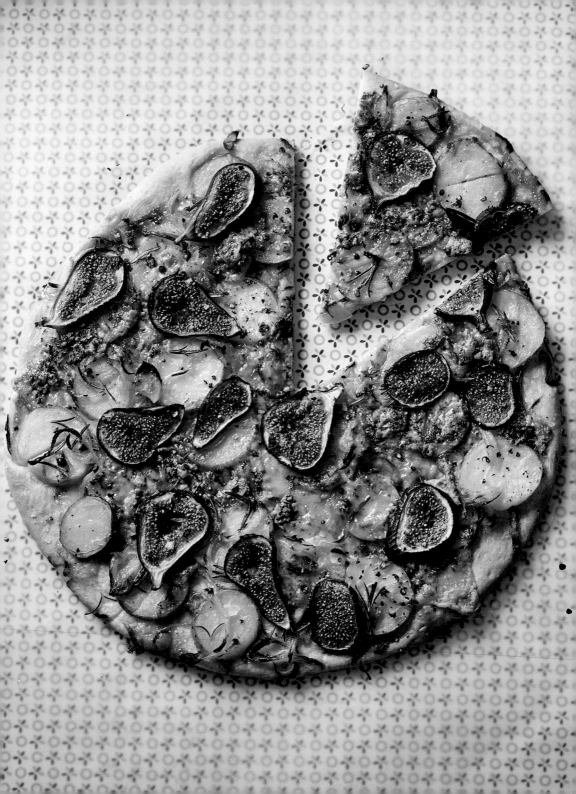

★ ★

POTATO, GORGONZOLA, ROSEMARY & FIG PIZZAS

continued...

For the topping:
400g (14oz) waxy potatoes, such
    as Charlotte
4 tbsp olive oil
1 large onion, finely sliced
1 large garlic clove, finely chopped
handful of small rosemary sprigs
200g (7oz) Gorgonzola
4 small figs, sliced
sea salt and freshly ground
    black pepper

Meanwhile, put the oil in a large non-stick frying or
sauté pan and add the onion, garlic and rosemary.
Sauté over a medium–low heat until the onions are
soft but not coloured. Slice the potatoes and add
them to the mixture, stirring them gently to coat
in the oil but being careful not to break them up.
Season with salt and pepper and set aside.

Once ready to cook, roll out the dough on a lightly
floured surface to a circle as thin as you possibly
can and about 30cm (12in) wide. Quickly remove
the stone from the oven and sprinkle it with flour.
Transfer the dough to the stone and spoon half the
potato topping over the dough, spreading it out.
Crumble over half the Gorgonzola and top with
half the fig slices. Bake the pizza for about
12 minutes, until the dough is cooked and crisp
and the cheese is melted. Serve while you repeat
to cook the second pizza.

POTATO, CORN &
★
CORIANDER CAKES

These make a great veggie main, and the perfect base
for the chunky, fresh avocado and lime salsa.

SERVES 4

TAKES 45 minutes

For the potato cakes:
1kg (2lb 4oz) floury potatoes,
  peeled
40g (1½oz/2½ tbsp) butter
3 tbsp milk
1 x 198g (7oz) can sweetcorn,
  drained
8 spring onions (scallions), sliced
1 tsp ground cumin
small bunch of coriander (cilantro)
  leaves, roughly chopped
about 60g (2oz/½ cup) plain
  (all-purpose) flour
2 eggs, beaten
100g (3½oz/1 cup) dried
  breadcrumbs
vegetable or sunflower oil,
  for frying
¼ tsp fine sea salt
freshly ground black pepper

Cut the potatoes into even-sized chunks, put them
in a pan and cover with cold, salted water. Bring
to the boil, cover, then lower the heat and simmer
for about 15 minutes, or until very tender.

While the potatoes are cooking, make the salsa. Put
all the ingredients in a bowl and mix to combine.

Drain the cooked potatoes in a colander, then
return them to the hot pan and mash with the
butter and milk until smooth. Season well with the
salt and pepper.

Stir the sweetcorn, spring onions (scallions), cumin
and coriander (cilantro) into the mash, then divide
it into 8 even portions. Shape each one into a patty
about 2cm (¾in) thick.

Put the flour on a plate, the eggs in a shallow bowl
and the breadcrumbs on another plate. One at a
time, dip the patties into the flour, then cover in
the egg, then coat completely in breadcrumbs.

POTATO, CORN & CORIANDER CAKES
continued...

For the salsa:
2 avocados, peeled, pitted and
    roughly diced
100g (3½oz) tomatoes (mixed
    colours), roughly chopped
juice of 1 lime and zest of ½ lime
1 red chilli, deseeded and finely
    diced (leave the seeds in if you
    want the salsa hotter)
½ tbsp olive oil
large handful of coriander
    (cilantro) leaves, roughly
    chopped

Heat about 1cm (½in) depth of oil in a frying pan. Once hot, add the patties to the pan and fry for 3–4 minutes on each side, until golden and crisp. You may need to do this in batches, depending on the size of your pan. Once cooked, remove the cakes from the pan with a spatula and let drain on kitchen paper for a few seconds before transferring to plates and piling the salsa on top, to serve.

COTTAGE PIES
★
IN COATS

A fun take on the classic cottage pie that really makes the potato the star of the show.

🍴 SERVES 4

⏰ TAKES 1¾ hours

4 large baking potatoes
3 tbsp whole milk
30g (1oz/2 tbsp) butter
75g (2½oz/¾ cup) grated
    Cheddar cheese

For the filling:
2 tbsp olive oil
1 onion, finely diced
1 carrot, peeled and finely diced
1 celery stick, finely diced
500g (1lb 2oz) minced
    (ground) beef
100ml (3½fl oz/scant ½ cup)
    red wine
1 x 400g (14oz) can chopped
    tomatoes
400ml (14fl oz/1¾ cups) beef stock
1 tbsp tomato purée (paste)
2 tbsp Worcestershire sauce
1 tsp dried thyme
sea salt and freshly ground
    black pepper

Preheat the oven to 180ºC/350ºF/gas 4. Bake the potatoes for 1–1½ hours, or until very tender.

Meanwhile, make the filling. Heat the oil in a large saucepan set over low heat and sauté the onion, carrot and celery for 10 minutes until soft. Turn the heat up to medium, add the beef and cook for a few minutes until it is browned. Add the red wine and cook until almost all of the liquid has gone, then add the chopped tomatoes and beef stock. Add the tomato purée (paste), Worcestershire sauce and thyme and stir everything together. Let the sauce simmer away for 30 minutes, uncovered, until it is rich and thickened, stirring every few minutes so it doesn't stick. Season to taste.

Remove the cooked potatoes from the oven and turn the oven up to 200ºC/400ºF/gas 6. Slice the potatoes in half lengthwise, scoop out all the insides with a spoon, being careful not to break the skins, and put it in a mixing bowl. Add the milk, butter and seasoning, and mash until smooth.

Place the potato skins on a baking tray and divide the filling evenly between the 8 jackets. Spread mashed potato over the top of each one. Sprinkle the tops of the potatoes with the cheese and return to the oven for 10 minutes or so, until the cheese is melted and turning golden.

GNOCCHI WITH MUSHROOMS
★
& TARRAGON

If you're in a hurry, you can skip the frying the gnocchi
step and just add it straight to the sauce, but a little golden
crispness does make it taste even better.

SERVES 4

TAKES 25 minutes, plus
making the gnocchi

1 tbsp olive oil, plus a drizzle extra
    for the gnocchi
600g (1lb 5oz) mixed mushrooms,
    sliced or halved
1 onion, finely sliced
2 large garlic cloves, finely
    chopped
175ml (5½fl oz/¾ cup) white wine
150ml (5fl oz/scant ⅔ cup) double
    (heavy) cream
1 tsp wholegrain mustard
a few stalks of tarragon, leaves
    picked and chopped
1 recipe quantity Gnocchi
    (see page 18)
sea salt and freshly ground
    black pepper

Put a large saucepan of salted water on the hob to
start bringing it to the boil.

Heat the oil in a large frying or sauté pan over a
high heat. Add the mushrooms to the pan and cook
until beginning to pick up some colour (you may
need to add them in batches, waiting for one batch
to wilt down before you have space to add the
next). Lower the heat to medium–low and add the
onion and garlic. Cook for 5–6 minutes until the
onion is softened and translucent.

Add the wine to the pan and let it cook for a
few minutes until it has reduced to about half its
volume. Add the cream, mustard and tarragon, then
stir together and season.

Cook the gnocchi in batches as per the instructions
on page 18. Once cooked, drain the gnocchi in a
colander, then transfer to a bowl and coat lightly
with oil to stop it sticking together.

Heat a non-stick frying pan over a medium–heat
and, again working in batches, fry the gnocchi until
beginning to turn golden and crisp on the outside.

Tip the gnocchi into the sauce, stir everything
together and serve immediately.

GNOCCHI
★
SALMON BAKE

Delicious fresh, leftover gnocchi are also great warmed up,
when they become a slightly different dish. These twice-
baked gnocchi really crisp up and turn golden from the hot
dish. It might even be even better the next day...

 SERVES 4

TAKES 40 minutes

butter, for greasing
1 slice of white bread, blitzed
    into breadcrumbs
1 recipe quantity Gnocchi
    (see page 18)
200g (7oz) long-stem broccoli
140g (5oz) fresh pesto
350g (12oz) hot smoked salmon
zest of 1 lemon
sea salt and freshly ground
    black pepper

Preheat the oven to 180ºC/350ºF/gas 4 and grease
a 20cm (8in) square baking dish with butter. Mix a
little seasoning into the breadcrumbs and set aside.

Get a pan of salted water boiling, and cook the
gnocchi as per the recipe on page 18. Work in
batches, fishing out the gnocchi with a slotted
spoon when it floats to the surface. Pop them in a
colander and let them drain, then transfer to a large
bowl, drizzle with a little oil and mix around to
stop them sticking together. Don't do this too far
in advance as you want the gnocchi to be slightly
warm when it goes into the oven, not stone cold.

Use the same water to quickly blanch the broccoli
for just 1½ minutes, then drain in the colander. Add
the broccoli to the gnocchi, then mix in the pesto
until everything is well coated. Flake the salmon
into the bowl and do a couple of gentle folds to
combine – don't break it up too much.

Tip all this into the prepared baking dish and
sprinkle the breadcrumbs over the top. Transfer to
the oven and bake for about 20 minutes. Sprinkle
the lemon zest over the top and return to the oven
for 5 minutes, until everything is reheated and the
breadcrumbs are turning golden.

FENNEL, POTATO &
★
PANCETTA GRATINS

These gorgeous gratins pack in double fennel flavours for
huge fans – in the sliced bulbs and in the punchy seeds.
Use the very best pancetta you can find – from a
good deli, if you can stretch to it.

SERVES 4

TAKES 1 hour

1 tbsp olive oil
200g (7oz) smoked pancetta, diced
2 tsp fennel seeds
300ml (10½fl oz/1¼ cups) double
   (heavy) cream
150ml (5fl oz/scant ⅔ cup)
   whole milk
butter, for greasing
900g (2lb) potatoes, peeled
   and sliced very thinly on a
   mandoline
2 fennel bulbs, sliced very thinly
   on a mandoline
80g (2¾oz/scant 1 cup) grated
   Gruyère cheese
sea salt and freshly ground
   black pepper

Preheat the oven to 180ºC/350ºF/gas 4.

Heat the oil in a heavy-based frying pan over a
medium heat and add the pancetta and fennel
seeds. Cook for about 5 minutes, or until the
pancetta is beginning to turn a golden brown.
Remove the pan from the heat.

In a jug, combine the cream and milk. Season with
a little salt (the pancetta will be quite salty) and
plenty of black pepper.

Grease 4 individual-sized baking dishes with butter.
Spread one-third of the potato slices evenly over
the base. Top with half of the fennel slices and
half of the pancetta and fennel seed mixture. Pour
over one-third of the cream mixture. Repeat to
add another layer of potato, the remaining fennel
slices and the remaining pancetta, then pour over
another one-third of the cream. Top with the final
one-third of potatoes and pour over the remaining
cream. Sprinkle cheese over the top of each dish.

Bake for about 50 minutes, or until the vegetables
feel tender all the way through when a knife is
inserted, and the cheese on top is golden.

SWEET POTATO, COCONUT & GREENS CURRY

Use morning glory for this red Thai-style curry, if you can find it, for a touch more authenticity, otherwise, spinach works just as well.

 SERVES 4

TAKES 40 minutes

2 tbsp oil
1 large onion, diced
3 large garlic cloves, finely chopped
a chunky 5cm (2in) piece fresh ginger, peeled and grated
1–2 red chillies, finely sliced
1 tbsp lemongrass paste
1½ tsp ground cumin
1½ tsp ground coriander
1½ tsp paprika
2–3 large sweet potatoes (about 900g/2lb total weight), peeled and diced into 2cm (¾in) chunks
2 x 400g (14oz) cans coconut milk
300g (10oz/6 7 cups) oriental greens, such as morning glory, or spinach leaves
a squeeze of lime juice
sea salt
jasmine rice, to serve

Heat the oil in a large saucepan over medium–low heat. Add the onion and sauté for 5 minutes until softened. Add the garlic, ginger, chilli, lemongrass paste and dried spices and cook for a couple of minutes more, until everything is smelling aromatic.

Add the sweet potato chunks to the pan and stir them around to coat them in the spices. Cook for a couple of minutes before adding the cans of coconut milk. Bring the liquid to a simmer and leave to bubble away gently, uncovered, for about 25 minutes until the sweet potato is really tender. Give it a stir every now and then to make sure nothing is sticking to the base of the pan.

Once the potato is tender, stir in the morning glory or spinach leaves and cook for just a couple of minutes until it is wilted into the curry. Taste and season with lime juice and salt, then serve with rice.

REUBENS

★

TARTIFLETTE

The classic après-ski feast given a twist. Just switch the bacon for salt beef and add some mustard and gherkins for the ultimate in fusion comfort food.

🍴 SERVES 4–6

⏰ TAKES 35 minutes

30g (1oz/2 tbsp) butter, plus
  extra for greasing
900g (2lb) Désirée potatoes,
  unpeeled and halved if
  very large
1 tbsp olive oil
1 large onion, finely sliced
2 large garlic cloves, finely
  chopped
90ml (3fl oz/6 tbsp) white wine
125ml (4fl oz/½ cup) single
  (light) cream
1½ tbsp French's American
  mustard
200g (7oz) salt beef, chopped
  into chunks
a half moon of Reblochon cheese
  (about 250g/9oz)
70g (2½oz) cornichons, sliced
sea salt and freshly ground
  black pepper
green salad, to serve

Preheat the oven to 200°C/400°F/gas 6 and grease a 20cm (8in) square baking dish with butter.

Cook the potatoes in a pan of salted water for about 15 minutes, or until tender but still quite firm – about a minute or so off being perfectly done.

Meanwhile, melt the butter in a large saucepan with the oil over medium–low heat and add the onion. Sauté for 5 minutes, then add the garlic and cook for another 5 minutes. Add the wine and cook until almost all of the liquid has gone, then add the cream and mustard, stir together and turn the heat off. Taste and season with salt and pepper.

Once the potatoes are almost done, drain them in a colander and leave them until cool enough to handle. Chop them into large chunks and tip them into the creamy mustard sauce. Stir together gently.

Spread half the potato mixture over the base of the baking dish, then scatter over the salt beef. Top with the remaining potato mix. Slice the Reblochon half moon horizontally and place the two halves on top of the potatoes, rind side down. Bake for 12–15 minutes until the cheese is melted and turning golden. Sprinkle over a few of the cornichons, then serve immediately with the remaining cornichons and a green salad on the side, for balance.

HOMITY

★

PIE

This classic user-upper dish has a nostalgic between-the-wars feel. Not that it makes it any less satisfying – or indulgent.

SERVES 4–6

TAKES 1 hour

375g (13oz) sheet of ready-rolled shortcrust pastry
650g (1lb 7oz) floury potatoes, peeled and cut into chunks
30g (1oz/2 tbsp) butter
1 tbsp olive oil
1 large onion, sliced
2 leeks, sliced
1 garlic clove, finely chopped
leaves stripped from a few thyme sprigs
75ml (2¼fl oz/5 tbsp) double (heavy) cream
150g (5½oz/1½ cups) grated Cheddar cheese
sea salt and freshly ground black pepper

Preheat the oven to 190ºC/375ºF/gas 5.

Use the pastry sheet to line a 23cm (9in) pie plate, then chill it for 20 minutes. Fill the pastry case with baking parchment and baking beans and blind bake for 10 minutes. Remove the parchment and beans and bake for another 12 minutes or so until the base is light golden.

While the pastry is chilling and cooking, prepare the filling. Put the potatoes in a pan of cold, salted water and bring them to the boil over high heat. Turn the heat down a little and simmer for about 15 minutes, or until tender but still quite firm – about a minute or so off being perfectly done.

Meanwhile, melt the butter with the oil in a large frying or sauté pan over medium–low heat and add the onion, leeks, garlic and thyme leaves. Fry gently for 10–15 minutes, stirring frequently and not letting anything colour, until everything is meltingly tender.

★ ★

HOMITY PIE
continued...

Once the potatoes are cooked, drain them and leave them to steam dry in the colander for a couple of minutes. Add them to the pan with the onions, then add the cream and three-quarters of the cheese. Stir everything around gently, being careful not to break up the potato, and season well with salt and pepper.

Once the pastry is blind baked, pile the filling into the pastry case. Sprinkle the remaining cheese over the top and return the pie to the oven for about 15 minutes, or until the cheese on top is melted and golden.

LANCASHIRE

★

HOTPOT

An oldie but definitely a goodie. A rich meat stew, covered in a cosy blanket of golden roasted potato – this is exactly what's needed on dreary days.

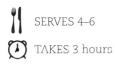

SERVES 4–6

TAKES 3 hours

3 tbsp sunflower oil
800g (1lb 12oz) braising lamb, chopped into large bite-sized chunks
4 lamb's kidneys, cored and roughly chopped
80g (2¾oz/⅓ cup) butter
2 onions, finely sliced
500ml (17fl oz/2 cups) lamb stock
1 tbsp Worcestershire sauce
leaves from 4 bushy sprigs of thyme
2 tablespoons chopped rosemary needles
2 bay leaves
1 large carrot, peeled and diced
1 tablespoon cornflour (cornstarch)
700g (1lb 8oz) potatoes, peeled and sliced into 3–4mm/⅛in thick slices on a mandoline
sea salt and freshly ground black pepper

Put 1 tablespoon of the oil in a shallow casserole and fry half of the lamb steak chunks for a few minutes until picking up a good colour all over. Remove from the pan and add another 1 tablespoon of oil and cook the remaining lamb in the same way. Remove from the pan and add the final 1 tablespoon of oil and the lamb's kidneys. Cook for a few minutes until browned, then add to a bowl with the rest of the lamb.

Put half the butter into the pan and fry the onions over a low–medium heat for about 10 minutes until softened and beginning to brown and caramelize. Pour in the stock and return the lamb to the pan, along with any juices that have collected in the bowl. Add the Worcestershire sauce and herbs and season with a bit of salt and pepper. Cook for 45 minutes with lid on, then remove the lid and add the carrots. Dissolve the cornflour (cornstarch) in a tablespoon of water and stir this into the casserole, too. Cook for a further 30 minutes with the lid on the pan. The gravy needs to be thick enough that the potatoes don't sink into it, but if you think it's thickening too much and starting to catch, add a splash of water. Taste and adjust the seasoning, if needs be.

★ ★

LANCASHIRE HOTPOT
continued...

Meanwhile, preheat the oven to 180°C/350°F/gas 4.

When the casserole has reduced to your liking, remove it from the heat and arrange the potato slices neatly over the top. Melt the remaining butter and brush it over the potatoes. Put the hotpot in the oven and bake for 45 minutes–1 hour until the potatoes are cooked through. If it looks like the potatoes are going a little too brown, remove the dish from the oven and cover it with foil so that they don't get any darker. You might want to brush a little more butter over the potatoes as you do this so that they get really golden and crisp. Take the dish straight to the table to serve.

PINK POTATO & SAUSAGE ★ TRAY BAKE

Let's be clear – you definitely don't want the middles of your sausages to be pink here. The hue is referring to the lovely beetroot, which tends to stain everything in its wake a pretty pink.

SERVES 4

TAKES 1¼ hours

500g (1lb 2oz) small beetroots (beets)
800g (1lb 12oz) baby new potatoes, halved
a good glug of olive oil
2 large red onions, peeled and each cut into 6 wedges
8 good-quality pork sausages (if you use cheap ones here, the tray may end up swimming in fat, so splash out on nice ones)
a good few thyme sprigs
4 garlic cloves, unpeeled but bashed
sea salt and freshly ground black pepper

Preheat the oven to 190ºC/375ºF/gas 5.

Put the whole beetroots (beets) in a pan of cold water and bring to the boil. Cook for 10–15 minutes until softening, but still quite firm. Drain, and once cool enough to handle, slip the skins off under running water, then halve them.

Put the cooked beetroot and the potatoes in a large roasting pan and drizzle over some olive oil. Mix everything around so all the veg are coated in the oil and add a sprinkle of salt. Roast for 20–25 minutes, until everything is starting to soften.

Add the onion wedges, sausages, thyme sprigs and garlic to the pan and, again, stir around to coat everything in the oil. Don't be tempted to add loads of extra oil here, as the sausages will release a fair bit of fat. Return the pan to the oven and roast for another 25–30 minutes, stirring halfway through, until the veg are soft and tender and the sausages are golden and cooked through.

Sprinkle over a bit of salt and a grind of black pepper and serve.

SWEET POTATO & BEAN
★
CHILLI TACOS

Serve this in tacos with all the usual trimmings – lettuce,
cheese, soured cream – whatever you fancy. It makes quite
a big pan, but freezes well.

SERVES 4–6

TAKES 40 minutes

3 tbsp olive oil
1 large onion, diced
3 garlic cloves, finely chopped
1 red chilli, finely diced (deseed
    if you want it milder)
1 tsp ground cumin
2 tsp sweet smoked paprika
½ tsp ground cinnamon
½–1 tsp cayenne pepper
2 star anise
700g (1lb 8oz) sweet potatoes,
    peeled and diced into 2cm
    (¾in) chunks
2 x 400g (14oz) cans chopped
    tomatoes
1 tbsp tomato purée (paste)
1 x 400g (14oz) can red kidney
    beans
1 x 400g (14oz) can black-eyed
    beans
2 jarred, roasted red peppers,
    drained, rinsed and sliced
1 tbsp dark soft brown sugar
sea salt and freshly ground
    black pepper

Heat the oil in a large saucepan and add the onion.
Sauté for about 5 minutes, until beginning to
soften. Add the garlic, red chilli and dried spices
and cook for another couple of minutes.

Add the sweet potatoes to the pan and stir so
they're coated in the spiced oil. Tip in a can of
tomatoes, then fill the can about one-third full with
water, swill it around and tip it into the pan. Do the
same with the second can, then stir in the tomato
purée (paste).

Bring the liquid to a simmer and cook for about 20
minutes, uncovered, until the sweet potato is very
close to tender and the sauce is thickened. Keep an
eye on it and stir frequently and if it starts to catch,
add a splash more water.

Pick out the two star anise and discard, then add
the beans, red peppers and brown sugar to the
pan. Stir in and cook for a further 5 minutes until
the sweet potato is completely tender. Taste and
season with salt and pepper.

Serve the chilli with tacos and all the usual
trimmings and let people build their own.

NEW POTATO, CHICKEN &
OLIVE TAGINE

Potatoes lend themselves well to tagines, absorbing all the flavours as the tagine cooks, and adding the substance the dish needs to make it a perfect one-pot dinner.

SERVES 4

TAKES 45 minutes

3 tbsp olive oil
8 skinless, boneless chicken thighs
1 tsp cumin seeds
1½ tsp coriander seeds
1½ tsp ras-el-hanout
1 tsp dried thyme
1 large onion, sliced
3 large garlic cloves, chopped
2.5cm (1in) piece of fresh ginger, peeled and finely chopped
600g (1lb 5oz) baby potatoes, halved if large
400ml (14fl oz/1¾ cups) hot chicken stock
1 red (bell) pepper, deseeded and sliced
1 green (bell) pepper, deseeded and sliced
200g (7oz) green beans, trimmed
2 tbsp olive oil
120g (4oz/1 cup) large green olives
finely diced peel from ½ preserved lemon (discard the flesh)
sea salt and freshly ground black pepper

Heat the olive oil in a large casserole dish over a high heat and, working in batches, brown the chicken thighs. Remove from the pan, leaving the fat in the pan, and set aside.

Turn the heat down to low and add the cumin and coriander seeds to the casserole. Cook for a couple of minutes until they are smelling aromatic. Add the ras-el-hanout and thyme and cook for a few seconds before adding the onion. Cook for 5 minutes, then add the garlic and ginger and cook for 3 minutes more.

Add the potatoes to the pan and stir to coat in the spiced oil. Add the stock, then place the browned chicken thighs on top. Cover the pan loosely with a lid and bring the stock to the boil, then reduce the heat to a simmer and cook the tagine for 15 minutes, or until the chicken and potatoes are almost cooked.

Carefully move the chicken aside and stir in the peppers, green beans, olives and preserved lemon. Replace the chicken on top and cook for another 10 minutes or so, until the potatoes are tender and the chicken is cooked through. Season with salt and pepper and serve.

PLENTIFUL-POTATO
★
TUNA NIÇOISE

Ramping up the potatoes in this dish takes it from 'salad' to 'satisfying' in one easy step.

SERVES 4

TAKES 20 minutes

800g (1lb 12oz) baby new potatoes
325g (11oz) green beans
4 eggs (at room temperature)
200g (7oz) cherry tomatoes (at room temp, not straight from the fridge), halved
1 x 100g (3½oz) jar anchovy fillets
75g (2½oz/¾ cup) good-quality pitted black olives, halved
2 tbsp drained baby capers
drizzle of olive oil
4 fresh tuna steaks

For the dressing:
4 tbsp extra virgin olive oil
1 tbsp grainy mustard
2 tbsp red wine vinegar
1 small garlic clove, crushed
sea salt and freshly ground black pepper

Cook the potatoes for 10–12 minutes in boiling, salted water, or until tender when pierced with a knife. In a separate pan, blanch the beans in boiling, salted water for about 4 minutes until bright green and tender, but still with a little crunch.

Meanwhile, boil the eggs for 5½ minutes – the whites will be set but the yolks still soft. Run them under cold water to stop them cooking further. When cool, peel and cut them in half lengthways.

Combine all the ingredients for the dressing in a small jug and whisk together. Season well.

Put the cooked potatoes in a salad bowl and add the beans, tomatoes, anchovies, olives and capers. Add the dressing and toss everything together.

Preheat a ridged griddle pan over very high heat. Rub the tuna steaks with oil and season them. When the pan is very hot, put the tuna steaks on it (they should sizzle) and cook for about 1 minute on each side (longer if they are quite thick), until char marks appear on the outside, but the tuna is still pink in the middle.

Cut the tuna into thick slices and arrange over the salad. Add the egg halves on top and serve.

PORTUGUESE POTATO &
★
SQUID STEW

This fresh, seafoody stew makes the perfect summer dinner. If you have smoked sea salt, try adding it to this. Or for a real kick, use hot smoked paprika rather than sweet.

 SERVES 4

TAKES 1 hour

4 tbsp olive oil
800g (1lb 12oz) cleaned squid, cut into rings (or lengths, for the tentacles)
3 garlic cloves, finely chopped
2 red (bell) peppers, deseeded and diced
175ml (5½fl oz/¾ cup) white wine
450ml (16fl oz/2 cups) good fish stock
800g (1lb 12oz) fresh ripe tomatoes, peeled and roughly chopped
1 tbsp tomato purée (paste)
1 tbsp sweet smoked paprika
800g (1lb 12oz) new potatoes, peeled and cut into 4cm (1½in) chunks
leaves from a small bunch of flat-leaf parsley, chopped
sea salt and freshly ground black pepper

Heat the oil in a large saucepan over high heat. Add the squid and cook until it's picking up some colour (you'll probably need to do this in batches). Turn the heat down to medium–low and add the onions. Cook for 5 minutes until they are beginning to soften, then add the garlic and the peppers and cook for a few minutes more.

Add the wine to the pan and turn up the heat a little. Cook for a few minutes until the liquid is reduced to about half its volume, then add the stock, tomatoes, tomato purée (paste) and paprika. Cook for about 20 minutes, uncovered, at a gentle simmer, until the liquid is starting to reduce to a thicker sauce and the squid is starting to tenderize.

Add the potatoes to the pan and simmer for another 40 minutes, or until the potatoes are really tender. If all the sauce is disappearing, cover the pan with a lid.

Taste and season with salt and black pepper, and stir in the parsley just before serving.

LOMO

★

SALTADO

An elegant-sounding title for a chip and steak stir-fry – and,
just so you know, it is as good as it sounds.

SERVES 4

TAKES 20 minutes

5 tbsp soy sauce
2 tbsp red wine vinegar
2 tsp ground cumin
800g (1lb 12oz) sirloin steak,
　sliced into strips
2 tbsp olive oil
1 red onion, finely sliced
1 red (bell) pepper, deseeded
　and sliced
1 green (bell) pepper, deseeded
　and sliced
4 tomatoes, deseeded and sliced
small bunch of coriander
　(cilantro), roughly chopped
½ recipe quantity Chips
　(see page 16)
sea salt and freshly ground
　black pepper

In a small bowl, combine the soy sauce, vinegar and
cumin and set aside.

Season the steak with salt and pepper. Heat the oil
in a wok over a high heat until very hot. Add half
the steak and quickly flash fry until browned on the
outside but still quite pink in the middle. Fish the
cooked steak out with a slotted spoon, leaving the
oil in the wok and repeat to cook the second half
of the steak. Remove that from the wok, too, and
set aside.

Turn the heat down and let the wok cool for a
minute or so. Add the red onion to the wok and
cook for a couple of minutes until softening. Add
the red and green peppers and give it a couple
more minutes. Add the tomatoes and soy mixture
and let it cook for a couple more minutes, until the
liquid is reduced a little, the tomatoes are soft and
until everything is almost tender (although a bit of
crunch still in the peppers is nice).

Quickly return the steak to the wok, and stir it in,
along with most of the coriander (cilantro). Add
the chips and give the mixture a couple more stirs
before serving immediately in the wok with the
remaining coriander sprinkled over the top.

INDEX

★★★★★★★★★★★★★★★★★★★★★★★★★★★★★★★★★★★★★

ACKNOWLEDGEMENTS

Thanks to Céline, Katherine and everyone else at Quadrille who had a hand in making this book.

Cheers to Faith for lovely photography, Alex for perfect propping, and Emma and other Alex for kitchen back-up.

And, finally, thanks to all those family, friends and neighbours who humoured me upon opening the front door to find me there clutching yet another foil-covered baking dish. Your insightful feedback and insatiable appetite for spuds saw me through.

ABOUT THE AUTHOR

★

Rebecca Woods is an author, food stylist and recipe developer. She spent many years editing cookery books before deciding she would much rather be cooking. Her styling work has appeared in the national press, film and TV, and brand advertising campaigns, as well as in many cookbooks.